ROMEO AND JULIET

WITH READER'S GUIDE

AMSCO LITERATURE PROGRAM

WILBERT J. LEVY, *Program Editor*

William Shakespeare

ROMEO AND JULIET

Amsco Literature Program

When ordering this book, you may specify:
R 32 ALP (Paperback)

WITH READER'S GUIDE

~~~~~~

Barbara Brandt

Teacher of English
Newtown High School
New York City

Amsco School Publications, Inc.

315 HUDSON STREET NEW YORK, N.Y. 10013

Please visit our web site at:

www.amscopub.com

ISBN 978-0-87720-821-1 (Paperback)

Romeo and Juliet with Reader's Guide

Copyright © 1974 by Amsco School Publications, Inc.

Printed in the United States of America

CONTENTS

Characters in the Play

Escalus, prince of Verona
Paris, a young nobleman, kinsman to the prince
Montague
Capulet } heads of two houses at variance with each other
An old man, of the Capulet family
Romeo, son to Montague
Mercutio, kinsman to the prince, and friend to Romeo
Benvolio, nephew to Montague, and friend to Romeo
Tybalt, nephew to Lady Capulet
Friar Laurence, a Franciscan
Friar John, of the same order
Balthasar, servant to Romeo
Sampson
Gregory } servants to Capulet
Peter, servant to Juliet's nurse
Abraham, servant to Montague
Apothecary
Three Musicians
Page, to Paris; another *Page*; an *Officer*

Lady Montague, wife to Montague
Lady Capulet, wife to Capulet
Juliet, daughter to Capulet
Nurse, to Juliet

Citizens of Verona; kinsfolk of both houses; Maskers, Guards, Watchmen, and *Attendants*

Chorus

Romeo and Juliet

1 **dignity** rank.

3 **mutiny** strife.

6 **star-cross'd** ill-fated.

THE PROLOGUE

Enter Chorus.

Chorus
Two households, both alike in dignity, *a*
  In fair Verona, where we lay our scene, *b*
From ancient grudge break to new mutiny, *a*
  Where civil blood makes civil hands unclean. *b*
From forth the fatal loins of these two foes *c*   5
  A pair of star-cross'd lovers take their life; *d*
Whose misadventur'd piteous overthrows *c*
  Do with their death bury their parents' strife. *d*
The fearful passage of their death-mark'd love, *E*
  And the continuance of their parents' rage, *F*   10
Which, but their children's end, nought could remove, *E*
  Is now the two hours' traffic of our stage; *F*
The which if you with patient ears attend, *G*
What here shall miss, our toil shall strive to mend. *G*

Sonnet - a 14 line poem with a specific rhyming scheme

3

Stage directions **bucklers**   small shields.

1 **carry coals**   suffer insults.

2 **colliers**   coal workers.

3 **an**   if.

4 **collar**   hangman's noose.

11 **take the wall**   insult; allowing someone to walk on the side of the street nearest the house walls was considered an extension of courtesy during the Renaissance (because the side of the walkway nearest the street was usually strewn with filth), while the opposite, forcing him away from the wall, was deemed insulting.

ACT I

Scene 1. Verona. A public place

*Enter Sampson and Gregory, of the house of Capulet,
with swords and bucklers.*

Sampson
Gregory, on my word, we'll not carry coals.

Gregory
No, for then we should be colliers.

Sampson
I mean, an we be in choler, we'll draw.

Gregory
Aye, while you live, draw your neck out o' the collar.

Sampson
I strike quickly, being moved.   5

Gregory
But thou art not quickly moved to strike.

Sampson
A dog of the house of Montague moves me.

Gregory
To move is to stir, and to be valiant is to stand:
therefore, if thou art moved, thou runn'st away.

Sampson
A dog of that house shall move me to stand: I will   10
take the wall of any man or maid of Montague's.

29 poor John salted, dried fish, considered to be inferior
fare.

Gregory

That shows thee a weak slave; for the weakest goes to
the wall.

Sampson

'Tis true; and therefore women, being the weaker
vessels, are ever thrust to the wall: therefore I will   15
push Montague's men from the wall and thrust his
maids to the wall.

Gregory

The quarrel is between our masters and us their men.

Sampson

'Tis all one, I will show myself a tyrant: when I have
fought with the men, I will be cruel with the maids; I   20
will cut off their heads.

Gregory

The heads of the maids?

Sampson

Aye, the heads of the maids, or their maidenheads;
take it in what sense thou wilt.

Gregory

They must take it in sense that feel it.   25

Sampson

Me they shall feel while I am able to stand: and 'tis
known I am a pretty piece of flesh.

Gregory

'Tis well thou art not fish; if thou hadst, thou hadst
been poor John. Draw thy tool; here comes two of the
house of Montagues.   30

Enter Abraham and Balthasar.

Sampson

My naked weapon is out: quarrel; I will back thee.

Gregory

How! turn thy back and run?

Sampson

Fear me not.

34 **marry**   indeed; derived from the oath "by the Virgin Mary."

37 **list**   please.

38 **bite my thumb**   a defiant, insulting gesture.

Gregory
No, marry; I fear thee!

Sampson
Let us take the law of our sides; let them begin.   35

Gregory
I will frown as I pass by, and let them take it as they
list.

Sampson
Nay, as they dare. I will bite my thumb at them; which
is a disgrace to them, if they bear it.

Abraham
Do you bite your thumb at us, sir?   40

Sampson
I do bite my thumb, sir.

Abraham
Do you bite your thumb at us, sir?

Sampson
[*Aside to Gregory*]   Is the law of our side, if I say aye?

Gregory
No.

Sampson
No, sir, I do not bite my thumb at you, sir; but I bite   45
my thumb, sir.

Gregory
Do you quarrel, sir?

Abraham
Quarrel, sir! no, sir.

Sampson
But if you do, sir, I am for you: I serve as good a man
as you.   50

Abraham
No better.

Sampson
Well, sir.
    Enter Benvolio.

Benvolio - peace keeper
Tybalt - instigator

57 **swashing**   crashing.

61 **heartless**   cowardly.
   hinds   menials.

67 **Have at thee**   be warned; on your guard.

68 **bills**   long-handled, ax-headed spears.
   partisans   broad-bladed spears.

Gregory
[*Aside to Sampson*]   Say "better": here comes one of
my master's kinsmen.

Sampson
Yes, better, sir.   55

Abraham
You lie.

Sampson
Draw, if you be men. Gregory, remember thy swashing
blow.

[*They fight.*

Benvolio
Part, fools!

|*Beating down their weapons.*
Put up your swords; you know not what you do.   60

   Enter Tybalt.

Tybalt
What, art thou drawn among these heartless hinds?
Turn thee, Benvolio, look upon thy death.

Benvolio
I do but keep the peace: put up thy sword,
Or manage it to part these men with me.

Tybalt
What, drawn, and talk of peace! I hate the word,   65
As I hate hell, all Montagues, and thee:
Have at thee, coward!

[*They fight.*

   *Enter several of both houses, who join the fray; then
   enter Citizens and Peace officers, with clubs.*

First Officer
Clubs, bills, and partisans! strike! beat them down!
Down with the Capulets! down with the Montagues!

73 **spite**   defiance.

82 **mistemper'd**   tempered for evil.

86 **thrice**   three times.

88 **beseeming**   suitable.

Enter old Capulet in his gown, and Lady Capulet.

Capulet
  What noise is this? Give me my long sword, ho!   70
Lady Capulet
  A crutch, a crutch! why call you for a sword?
Capulet
  My sword, I say! Old Montague is come,
  And flourishes his blade in spite of me.

Enter old Montague and Lady Montague.

Montague
  Thou villain Capulet!—Hold me not, let me go.
Lady Montague
  Thou shalt not stir one foot to seek a foe.   75

Enter Prince Escalus, with his train.

Prince
  Rebellious subjects, enemies to peace,
  Profaners of this neighbor-stained steel—
  Will they not hear? What, ho! you men, you beasts,
  That quench the fire of your pernicious rage
  With purple fountains issuing from your veins,   80
  On pain of torture, from those bloody hands
  Throw your mistemper'd weapons to the ground,
  And hear the sentence of your moved prince.
  Three civil brawls, bred of an airy word,
  By thee, old Capulet, and Montague,   85
  Have thrice disturb'd the quiet of our streets,
  And made Verona's ancient citizens
  Cast by their grave beseeming ornaments,
  To wield old partisans, in hands as old,
  Canker'd with peace, to part your canker'd hate: 90
  If ever you disturb our streets again,
  Your lives shall pay the forfeit of the peace.
  For this time, all the rest depart away:
  You, Capulet, shall go along with me;

99 **set this ancient quarrel now abroach** open the tap of enmity again.

107 **withal** thereby.

109 **part** side.

115 **drave** drove.

119 **ware** aware.
120 **covert** hiding place.
121 **affections** inclinations.

And, Montague, come you this afternoon,   95
To know our farther pleasure in this case,
To old Freetown, our common judgment place.
Once more, on pain of death, all men depart.
> [*Exeunt all but Montague, Lady
> Montague, and Benvolio.*

Montague
Who set this ancient quarrel new abroach?
Speak, nephew, were you by when it began?   100

Benvolio
Here were the servants of your adversary
And yours close fighting ere I did approach:
I drew to part them: in the instant came
The fiery Tybalt, with his sword prepar'd;
Which, as he breath'd defiance to my ears,   105
He swung about his head, and cut the winds,
Who, nothing hurt withal, hiss'd him in scorn:
While we were interchanging thrusts and blows,
Came more and more, and fought on part and part,
Till the prince came, who parted either part.   110

Lady Montague
O, where is Romeo? saw you him today?
Right glad I am he was not at this fray.

Benvolio
Madam, an hour before the worship'd sun
Peer'd forth the golden window of the east,
A troubled mind drave me to walk abroad;   115
Where, underneath the grove of sycamore
That westward rooteth from the city's side,
So early walking did I see your son:
Towards him I made; but he was ware of me,
And stole into the covert of the wood: 120
I, measuring his affections by my own,
Which then most sought where most might not be
    found,

131 **Aurora**   goddess of the dawn.
132 **heavy**   sorrowful.

upset over Rosaline

144 **close**   uncommunicative.
145 **sounding**   fathoming, being understood.
146 **envious**   malicious.

Being one too many by my weary self,
Pursu'd my humor, not pursuing his,
And gladly shunn'd who gladly fled from me. 125

Montague
Many a morning hath he there been seen,
With tears augmenting the fresh morning's dew,
Adding to clouds more clouds with his deep sighs:
But all so soon as the all-cheering sun
Should in the farthest east begin to draw 130
The shady curtains from Aurora's bed,
Away from light steals home my heavy son,
And private in his chamber pens himself,
Shuts up his windows, locks fair daylight out,
And makes himself an artificial night: 135
Black and portentous must this humor prove,
Unless good counsel may the cause remove.

Benvolio
My noble uncle, do you know the cause?

Montague
I neither know it nor can learn of him.

Benvolio
Have you importun'd him by any means? 140

Montague
Both by myself and many other friends:
But he, his own affections' counselor,
Is to himself—I will not say how true—
But to himself so secret and so close,
So far from sounding and discovery, 145
As is the bud bit with an envious worm
Ere he can spread his sweet leaves to the air,
Or dedicate his beauty to the sun.
Could we but learn from whence his sorrows grow,
We would as willingly give cure as know. 150

Enter Romeo.

153 **happy**   fortunate.
   stay   waiting.
154 **shrift**   confession.

155 **Good morrow**   good morning.

167 **proof**   experience.

168 **view is muffled still**   Cupid was often depicted as blind-folded.

Benvolio
See, where he comes: so please you step aside,
I'll know his grievance, or be much denied.

Montague
I would thou wert so happy by thy stay,
To hear true shrift. Come, madam, let's away.
                              [*Exeunt Montague and Lady.*

Benvolio
Good morrow, cousin.   155

Romeo
                              Is the day so young?

Benvolio
But new struck nine.

Romeo
                    Aye me! sad hours seem long.
Was that my father that went hence so fast?

Benvolio
It was. What sadness lengthens Romeo's hours?   160

Romeo
Not having that which, having, makes them short.

Benvolio
In love?

Romeo
Out—

Benvolio
Of love?

Romeo
Out of her favor, where I am in love.   165

Benvolio
Alas, that love, so gentle in his view,
Should be so tyrannous and rough in proof!

Romeo
Alas, that love, whose view is muffled still,
Should without eyes see pathways to his will!
Where shall we dine? O me! What fray was here?   170

175 **vanity**   frivolity.

178 **still-waking**   always wakeful.

181 **coz**   cousin.

186 **prest**   oppressed.

195 **Soft!**   Wait a moment!
196 **An if**   if.

198 **some other where**   somewhere else.

199 **sadness**   seriousness.

Yet tell me not, for I have heard it all.
Here's much to do with hate, but more with love:
Why, then, O brawling love! O loving hate!
O any thing, of nothing first create!
O heavy lightness! serious vanity!   175
Misshapen chaos of well-seeming forms!
Feather of lead, bright smoke, cold fire, sick health!
Still-waking sleep, that is not what it is!
This love feel I, that feel no love in this.
Dost thou not laugh?   180

Benvolio
           No, coz, I rather weep.

Romeo
Good heart, at what?

Benvolio
           At thy good heart's oppression.

Romeo
Why, such is love's transgression.
Griefs of mine own lie heavy in my breast;   185
Which thou wilt propagate, to have it prest
With more of thine: this love that thou hast shown
Doth add more grief to too much of mine own.
Love is a smoke rais'd with the fume of sighs;
Being purg'd, a fire sparkling in lovers' eyes;   190
Being vex'd, a sea nourish'd with lovers' tears:
What is it else? a madness most discreet,
A choking gall and a preserving sweet.
Farewell, my coz.

Benvolio
           Soft! I will go along: 195
An if you leave me so, you do me wrong.

Romeo
Tut, I have lost myself; I am not here;
This is not Romeo, he's some other where.

Benvolio
Tell me in sadness, who is that you love?

204 **ill urg'd**   inopportunely mentioned.

210 **Dian's wit**   the goddess Diana's wisdom to remain a virgin.
211 **proof**   armor.
213 **stay**   endure.

218 **still**   forever.

224 **forsworn to**   renounced.

Romeo
    What, shall I groan and tell thee?   200

Benvolio
                             Groan! why, no;
    But sadly tell me who.

Romeo
    Bid a sick man in sadness make his will:
    Ah, word ill urg'd to one that is so ill!
    In sadness, cousin, I do love a woman.   205

Benvolio
    I aim'd so near when I suppos'd you lov'd.

Romeo
    A right good markman! And she's fair I love.

Benvolio
    A right fair mark, fair coz, is soonest hit.

Romeo
    Well, in that hit you miss: she'll not be hit
    With Cupid's arrow; she hath Dian's wit,   210
    And in strong proof of chastity well arm'd,
    From love's weak childish bow she lives unharm'd.
    She will not stay the siege of loving terms,
    Nor bide the encounter of assailing eyes,
    Nor ope her lap to saint-seducing gold: 215
    O, she is rich in beauty, only poor
    That, when she dies, with beauty dies her store.

Benvolio
    Then she hath sworn that she will still live chaste?

Romeo
    She hath, and in that sparing makes huge waste;
    For beauty, starv'd with her severity,   220
    Cuts beauty off from all posterity.
    She is too fair, too wise, wisely too fair,
    To merit bliss by making me despair:
    She hath forsworn to love; and in that vow
    Do I live dead, that live to tell it now.   225

231 **call . . . in question**   contemplate.
232 **masks**   it was the custom for fashionable women to wear
masks on public occasions.

236 **passing**   surpassingly.

240 **pay that doctrine**   give that instruction.

4 **reckoning**   reputation.

Benvolio
　Be rul'd by me, forget to think of her.
Romeo
　O, teach me how I should forget to think.
Benvolio
　By giving liberty unto thine eyes;
　Examine other beauties.
Romeo
　　　　　　　'Tis the way　　　　　　　230
　To call hers, exquisite, in question more:
　These happy masks that kiss fair ladies' brows,
　Being black, put us in mind they hide the fair;
　He that is strucken blind cannot forget
　The precious treasure of his eyesight lost:　　235
　Show me a mistress that is passing fair,
　What doth her beauty serve but as a note
　Where I may read who pass'd that passing fair?
　Farewell: thou canst not teach me to forget.
Benvolio
　I'll pay that doctrine, or else die in debt.　　240

　　　　　　　　　　　　　　　[*Exeunt.*

Scene 2. A street

Enter Capulet, Paris, and Servant.

Capulet
　But Montague is bound as well as I,
　In penalty alike; and 'tis not hard, I think,
　For men so old as we to keep the peace.
Paris
　Of honorable reckoning are you both;
　And pity 'tis you liv'd at odds so long.　　5
　But now, my lord, what say you to my suit?

14 **The earth hath swallow'd all my hopes but she**   all of my
other children have died.

18 **An**   if.

22 **store**   gathering.

30 **Inherit**   possess.

34 **sirrah**   term of address to an inferior.

37 **on their pleasure stay**   awaits their pleasure.

Capulet
> But saying o'er what I have said before:
> My child is yet a stranger in the world;
> She hath not seen the change of fourteen years:
> Let two more summers wither in their pride   10
> Ere we may think her ripe to be a bride.

Paris
> Younger than she are happy mothers made.

Capulet
> And too soon marr'd are those so early made.
> The earth hath swallow'd all my hopes but she,
> She is the hopeful lady of my earth: 15
> But woo her, gentle Paris, get her heart;
> My will to her consent is but a part;
> An she agree, within her scope of choice
> Lies my consent and fair according voice.
> This night I hold an old accustom'd feast,   20
> Whereto I have invited many a guest,
> Such as I love; and you among the store,
> One more, most welcome, makes my number more.
> At my poor house look to behold this night
> Earth-treading stars that make dark heaven light: 25
> Such comfort as do lusty young men feel
> When well-apparel'd April on the heel
> Of limping winter treads, even such delight
> Among fresh female buds shall you this night
> Inherit at my house; hear all, all see,   30
> And like her most whose merit most shall be:
> Which on more view, of many mine being one
> May stand in number, though in reckoning none.
> Come, go with me. Go, sirrah, trudge about
> Through fair Verona; find those persons out   35
> Whose names are written there, and to them say,
> My house and welcome on their pleasure stay.
>   [*Exeunt Capulet and Paris.*

40 **yard**   measuring rod.
41 **pencil**   brush.

47 **holp**   helped.

51 **plantain leaf**   a medication.

57 **God-den**   good evening (used after noon).

Servant

Find them out whose names are written here! It is
written that the shoemaker should meddle with his
yard and the tailor with his last, the fisher with his   40
pencil and the painter with his nets; but I am sent to
find those persons whose names are here writ, and can
never find what names the writing person hath here
writ. I must to the learned. In good time.

    Enter Benvolio and Romeo.

Benvolio

Tut, man, one fire burns out another's burning.   45
    One pain is lessen'd by another's anguish;
Turn giddy, and be holp by backward turning;
    One desperate grief cures with another's languish:
Take thou some new infection to thy eye,
And the rank poison of the old will die.   50

Romeo

Your plantain leaf is excellent for that.

Benvolio

For what, I pray thee?

Romeo

                    For your broken shin.

Benvolio

Why, Romeo, art thou mad?

Romeo

Not mad, but bound more than a madman is;   55
Shut up in prison, kept without my food,
Whipt and tormented and—God-den, good fellow.

Servant

God gi' god-den. I pray, sir, can you read?

Romeo

Aye, mine own fortune in my misery.

Servant

Perhaps you have learned it without book: but, I pray,   60
can you read anything you see?

63 rest you merry! may you continue to be happy.

81 crush finish off.

Romeo
Aye, if I know the letters and the language.

Servant
Ye say honestly: rest you merry!

Romeo
Stay, fellow; I can read.

[*Reads.*

"Signior Martino and his wife and daughters; County   65
Anselme and his beauteous sisters; the lady widow of
Vitruvio; Signior Placentio and his lovely nieces; Mercutio and his brother Valentine; mine uncle Capulet,
his wife, and daughters; my fair niece Rosaline; Livia;
Signior Valentio and his cousin Tybalt; Lucio and the   70
lively Helena."

A fair assembly: whither should they come?

Servant
Up.

Romeo
Whither?

Servant
To supper; to our house.   75

Romeo
Whose house?

Servant
My master's.

Romeo
Indeed, I should have ask'd you that before.

Servant
Now I'll tell you without asking: my master is the
great rich Capulet; and if you be not of the house of   80
Montagues, I pray, come and crush a cup of wine.
Rest you merry!

[*Exit.*

Benvolio
At this same ancient feast of Capulet's

86 **unattainted** unbiased.

96 **pois'd** compared.

98 **lady's love** ladylove.

100 **scant** scarcely.

3 **ladybird** sweetheart.

Sups the fair Rosaline whom thou so lovest,
With all the admired beauties of Verona: 85
Go thither, and with unattainted eye
Compare her face with some that I shall show,
And I will make thee think thy swan a crow.

Romeo
When the devout religion of mine eye
    Maintains such falsehood, then turn tears to fires;   90
And these, who, often drown'd, could never die,
    Transparent heretics, be burnt for liars!
One fairer than my love! the all-seeing sun
Ne'er saw her match since first the world begun.

Benvolio
Tut, you saw her fair, none else being by,   95
Herself pois'd with herself in either eye:
But in that crystal scales let there be weigh'd
Your lady's love against some other maid,
That I will show you shining at this feast,
And she shall scant show well that now seems best.   100

Romeo
I'll go along, no such sight to be shown,
But to rejoice in splendor of mine own.
                                   [Exeunt.

Scene 3. A room in Capulet's house

Enter Lady Capulet and Nurse.

Lady Capulet
Nurse, where's my daughter? call her forth to me.
Nurse
Now, by my maidenhead at twelve year old,
I bade her come. What, lamb! what, ladybird!—
God forbid!—Where's this girl? What, Juliet!

8 **matter**   business.
   give leave   leave us.
10 **thou's**   thou shalt.
   counsel   secret consultation.
11 **pretty age**   ripe for marriage.

14 **lay**   wager.
15 **teen**   sorrow.

17 **Lammastide**   August 1, a harvest festival.

22 **of an age**   the same age.

25 **marry**   indeed.

29 **laid wormwood to my dug**   applied a bitter-tasting substance to her breast to facilitate weaning.

Enter Juliet.

Juliet
How now! who calls?   5

Nurse
Your mother.

Juliet
Madam, I am here. What is your will?

Lady Capulet
This is the matter. Nurse, give leave awhile,
We must talk in secret—nurse, come back again;
I have remember'd me, thou's hear our counsel.   10
Thou know'st my daughter's of a pretty age.

Nurse
Faith, I can tell her age unto an hour.

Lady Capulet
She's not fourteen.

Nurse
                          I'll lay fourteen of my teeth—
And yet, to my teen be it spoken, I have but four—   15
She is not fourteen. How long is it now
To Lammastide?

Lady Capulet
                          A fortnight and odd days.

Nurse
Even or odd, of all days in the year,
Come Lammas Eve at night shall she be fourteen.   20
Susan and she—God rest all Christian souls!—
Were of an age: well, Susan is with God;
She was too good for me: but, as I said,
On Lammas Eve at night shall she be fourteen;
That shall she, marry; I remember it well.   25
'Tis since the earthquake now eleven years;
And she was wean'd—I never shall forget it—
Of all the days of the year, upon that day:
For I had then laid wormwood to my dug,

32 **bear a brain**   keep my memory.

35 **tetchy**   fretful.
36 **I trow**   I assure you.

39 **high-lone**   quite alone.
   rood   cross.
41 **broke her brow**   cut her forehead.

43 **'A**   he.

45 **wit**   sense.
46 **by my holidame**   a mild oath.

51 **stinted**   stopped.

Sitting in the sun under the dove-house wall;   30
My lord and you were then at Mantua—
Nay, I do bear a brain—but, as I said,
When it did taste the wormwood on the nipple
Of my dug, and felt it bitter, pretty fool,
To see it tetchy, and fall out with the dug!   35
Shake, quoth the dove-house: 'twas no need, I trow,
To bid me trudge.
And since that time it is eleven years;
For then she could stand high-lone; nay, by the rood,
She could have run and waddled all about;   40
For even the day before, she broke her brow:
And then my husband—God be with his soul!
'A was a merry man—took up the child:
"Yea," quoth he, "dost thou fall upon thy face?
Thou wilt fall backward when thou hast more wit;   45
Wilt thou not, Jule?" and, by my holidame,
The pretty wretch left crying, and said "Aye."
To see now how a jest shall come about!
I warrant, an I should live a thousand years,
I never should forget it: "Wilt thou not, Jule?" quoth
    he;   50
And, pretty fool, it stinted, and said "Aye."

Lady Capulet
Enough of this; I pray thee, hold thy peace.

Nurse
Yes, madam: yet I cannot choose but laugh,
To think it should leave crying, and say "Aye":
And yet, I warrant, it had upon its brow   55
A bump as big as a young cock'rel's stone;
A perilous knock; and it cried bitterly:
"Yea," quoth my husband, "fall'st upon thy face?
Thou wilt fall backward when thou comest to age;
Wilt thou not, Jule?" it stinted, and said "Aye."   60

Juliet
And stint thou too, I pray thee, nurse, say I.

64 **once** someday.

79 **a man of wax** a model man (as beautiful as an artist's figure rendered in wax).

86 **married** harmonious.

Nurse
　　Peace, I have done. God mark thee to his grace!
　　Thou wast the prettiest babe that e'er I nurs'd:
　　An I might live to see thee married once,
　　I have my wish.   65

Lady Capulet
　　Marry, that "marry" is the very theme
　　I came to talk of. Tell me, daughter Juliet,
　　How stands your disposition to be married?

Juliet
　　It is an honor that I dream not of.

Nurse
　　An honor! were not I thine only nurse,   70
　　I would say thou hadst suck'd wisdom from my teat.

Lady Capulet
　　Well, think of marriage now; younger than you
　　Here in Verona, ladies of esteem,
　　Are made already mothers. By my count,
　　I was your mother much upon these years   75
　　That you are now a maid. Thus then in brief;
　　The valiant Paris seeks you for his love.

Nurse
　　A man, young lady! lady, such a man
　　As all the world—why, he's a man of wax.

Lady Capulet
　　Verona's summer hath not such a flower.   80

Nurse
　　Nay, he's a flower; in faith, a very flower.

Lady Capulet
　　What say you? can you love the gentleman?
　　This night you shall behold him at our feast:
　　Read o'er the volume of young Paris' face,
　　And find delight writ there with beauty's pen;   85
　　Examine every married lineament,
　　And see how one another lends content;

89 **margent**   margin.

99 **like of**   be pleased with.

105 **in extremity**   at the breaking point.
106 **straight**   immediately.

108 **county**   count.
    stays   awaits you.

And what obscur'd in this fair volume lies
Find written in the margent of his eyes.
This precious book of love, this unbound lover,   90
To beautify him, only lacks a cover:
The fish lives in the sea; and 'tis much pride
For fair without the fair within to hide:
That book in many's eyes doth share the glory,
That in gold clasps locks in the golden story: 95
So shall you share all that he doth possess,
By having him making yourself no less.

Nurse
No less! nay, bigger: women grow by men.

Lady Capulet
Speak briefly, can you like of Paris' love?

Juliet
I'll look to like, if looking liking move: 100
But no more deep will I endart mine eye
Than your consent gives strength to make it fly.

    Enter a Servingman.

Servingman
Madam, the guests are come, supper served up, you
called, my young lady asked for, the nurse cursed in the
pantry, and every thing in extremity. I must hence to   105
wait; I beseech you, follow straight.

Lady Capulet
We follow thee.

                    [*Exit Servingman.*
       Juliet, the county stays.

Nurse
Go, girl, seek happy nights to happy days.

                        [*Exeunt.*

1 **shall this speech be spoke for our excuse?** Shall we introduce our group of masked intruders formally? (as was customary).

4 **hoodwink'd** blindfolded.
5 **Tartar's painted bow** a bow whose shape resembles Cupid's.
6 **crowkeeper** an archer employed to scare away crows.
7 **without-book** memorized.
8 **After** with assistance from.
10 **measure them a measure** dance a stately dance with them.

12 **heavy** sad.

18 **bound** leap.

19 **sore-enpierced** painfully pierced.

21 **a pitch** that is, any distance at all.

Scene 4. A street

*Enter Romeo, Mercutio, Benvolio, with five or six
other Maskers, and Torchbearers.*

Romeo

    What, shall this speech be spoke for our excuse?
    Or shall we on without apology?

Benvolio

    The date is out of such prolixity:
    We'll have no Cupid hoodwink'd with a scarf,
    Bearing a Tartar's painted bow of lath,   5
    Scaring the ladies like a crowkeeper;
    Nor no without-book prologue, faintly spoke
    After the prompter, for our entrance:
    But, let them measure us by what they will,
    We'll measure them a measure, and be gone.   10

Romeo

    Give me a torch: I am not for this ambling;
    Being but heavy, I will bear the light.

Mercutio

    Nay, gentle Romeo, we must have you dance.

Romeo

    Not I, believe me: you have dancing shoes
    With nimble soles: I have a soul of lead   15
    So stakes me to the ground, I cannot move.

Mercutio

    You are a lover; borrow Cupid's wings,
    And soar with them above a common bound.

Romeo

    I am too sore-enpierced with his shaft,
    To soar with his light feathers, and so bound.   20
    I cannot bound a pitch above dull woe:
    Under love's heavy burden do I sink.

29 **case**   mask.
30 **a visor for a visor**   a mask for a masklike face.
31 **curious**   accurate.
   quote   observe.

35 **wantons**   triflers.
36 **senseless**   incapable of feeling.
   rushes   usual floor covering before carpets.
37 **proverb'd with a grandsire phrase**   counseled by an old
   proverb.

40 **dun's the mouse**   lie low, keep quiet (proverbial).
41 **Dun**   proverbial name for a horse.

43 **burn daylight**   waste time.

47 **good**   correct.

50 **wit**   wisdom.

Mercutio
> And, to sink in it, should you burden love;
> Too great oppression for a tender thing.

Romeo
> Is love a tender thing? it is too rough,   25
> Too rude, too boisterous, and it pricks like thorn.

Mercutio
> If love be rough with you, be rough with love;
> Prick love for pricking, and you beat love down.
> Give me a case to put my visage in:
> A visor for a visor! what care I   30
> What curious eye doth quote deformities?
> Here are the beetle-brows shall blush for me.

Benvolio
> Come, knock and enter, and no sooner in
> But every man betake him to his legs.

Romeo
> A torch for me: let wantons light of heart   35
> Tickle the senseless rushes with their heels;
> For I am proverb'd with a grandsire phrase;
> I'll be a candle-holder, and look on.
> The game was ne'er so fair, and I am done.

Mercutio
> Tut, dun's the mouse, the constable's own word: 40
> If thou art Dun, we'll draw thee from the mire
> Of this sir-reverence love, wherein thou stick'st
> Up to the ears. Come, we burn daylight, ho.

Romeo
> Nay, that's not so.

Mercutio
>   I mean, sir, in delay   45
> We waste our lights in vain, like lamps by day.
> Take our good meaning, for our judgment sits
> Five times in that ere once in our five wits.

Romeo
> And we mean well, in going to this mask;
> But 'tis no wit to go.   50

52 **tonight**   last night.

57 **Queen Mab**   queen of the fairies.

59 **agate stone**   a gem for a ring.

61 **atomies**   tiny creatures.

63 **spinners**   spiders.

72 **joiner**   cabinetmaker.

74 **state**   pomp.

78 **straight**   immediately.

Mercutio
                    Why, may one ask?

Romeo
  I dreamt a dream tonight.

Mercutio
                            And so did I.

Romeo
  Well, what was yours?

Mercutio
                        That dreamers often lie.   55

Romeo
  In bed asleep, while they do dream things true.

Mercutio
  O, then, I see Queen Mab hath been with you.
  She is the fairies' midwife, and she comes
  In shape no bigger than an agate stone
  On the forefinger of an alderman,   60
  Drawn with a team of little atomies
  Athwart men's noses as they lie asleep:
  Her wagon spokes made of long spinners' legs;
  The cover, of the wings of grasshoppers;
  Her traces, of the smallest spider's web;   65
  Her collars, of the moonshine's watery beams;
  Her whip, of cricket's bone; the lash, of film;
  Her wagoner, a small gray-coated gnat,
  Not half so big as a round little worm
  Prick'd from the lazy finger of a maid: 70
  Her chariot is an empty hazelnut,
  Made by the joiner squirrel or old grub,
  Time out o' mind the fairies' coachmakers.
  And in this state she gallops night by night
  Through lovers' brains, and then they dream of love;   75
  O'er courtiers' knees, that dream on curtsies straight;
  O'er lawyers' fingers, who straight dream on fees;
  O'er ladies' lips, who straight on kisses dream,

80 **sweetmeats**   breath fresheners.

83 **tithe-pig**   a pig paid to the parson as part of a parishioner's tax.

84 **'a**   he.

88 **ambuscadoes**   ambushes.

89 **anon**   presently.

94 **elflocks**   hair supposedly matted together by elves.

Which oft the angry Mab with blisters plagues,
Because their breaths with sweetmeats tainted are: 80
Sometime she gallops o'er a courtier's nose,
And then dreams he of smelling out a suit;
And sometime comes she with a tithe-pig's tail
Tickling a parson's nose as 'a lies asleep,
Then dreams he of another benefice: 85
Sometime she driveth o'er a soldier's neck,
And then dreams he of cutting foreign throats,
Of breaches, ambuscadoes, Spanish blades,
Of healths five fathoms deep; and then anon
Drums in his ear, at which he starts and wakes,   90
And being thus frighted swears a prayer or two,
And sleeps again. This is that very Mab
That plats the manes of horses in the night,
And bakes the elflocks in foul sluttish hairs,
Which once untangled much misfortune bodes: 95
This is the hag, when maids lie on their backs,
That presses them and learns them first to bear,
Making them women of good carriage:
This is she—

Romeo

    Peace, peace, Mercutio, peace!   100
Thou talk'st of nothing.

Mercutio

     True, I talk of dreams;
Which are the children of an idle brain,
Begot of nothing but vain fantasy,
Which is as thin of substance as the air,   105
And more inconstant than the wind, who woos
Even now the frozen bosom of the north,
And, being anger'd, puffs away from thence,
Turning his face to the dew-dropping south.

Benvolio

This wind you talk of blows us from ourselves;   110
Supper is done, and we shall come too late.

112 **misgives**   forbodes.

2 **trencher**   wooden platter.

5 **joint-stools**   sturdy stools made by cabinetmakers.
court-cupboard   sideboard.
6–7 **marchpane**   marzipan (a sweet dessert).

Romeo
    I fear, too early: for my mind misgives
    Some consequence, yet hanging in the stars,
    Shall bitterly begin his fearful date
    With this night's revels, and expire the term   115
    Of a despised life clos'd in my breast,
    By some vile forfeit of untimely death:
    But He, that hath the steerage of my course,
    Direct my sail! On, lusty gentlemen.

Benvolio
    Strike, drum.   120

                               [*Exeunt.*

Scene 5. *A hall in Capulet's house*

Musicians waiting. Enter Servingmen, with napkins.

First Servingman
    Where's Potpan, that he helps not to take away? he
    shift a trencher! he scrape a trencher!

Second Servingman
    When good manners shall lie all in one or two men's
    hands, and they unwashed too, 'tis a foul thing.

First Servingman
    Away with the joint-stools, remove the court-cupboard,   5
    look to the plate. Good thou, save me a piece of march-
    pane; and, as thou lovest me, let the porter let in Susan
    Grindstone and Nell. Antony, and Potpan!

Second Servingman
    Aye, boy, ready.

First Servingman
    You are looked for and called for, asked for and sought   10
    for, in the great chamber.

17 **makes dainty**   affects fastidiousness.
18 **come near ye now**   getting close to the truth.

24 **a hall**   clear the floor.

25 **knaves**   fellows.

27 **sirrah**   term of address used here to indicate familiarity.
28 **cousin**   any relative outside the immediate family.

32 **By'r Lady**   by Our Lady (the Virgin Mary).

35 **Pentecost**   seventh Sunday after Easter.

Third Servingman

We cannot be here and there too. Cheerly, boys; be
brisk a while, and the longer liver take all.

> [*They retire behind.*

> *Enter Capulet, with Juliet and others of his house,
> meeting the Guests and Maskers.*

Capulet

Welcome, gentlemen! ladies that have their toes
Unplagu'd with corns will have a bout with you: 15
Ah ha, my mistresses! which of you all
Will now deny to dance? She that makes dainty,
She, I'll swear, hath corns; am I come near ye now?
Welcome, gentlemen! I have seen the day
That I have worn a visor, and could tell   20
A whispering tale in a fair lady's ear,
Such as would please: 'tis gone, 'tis gone, 'tis gone:
You are welcome, gentlemen! Come musicians, play.
A hall, a hall! give room! and foot it, girls.

> [*Music plays, and they dance.*

More light, you knaves; and turn the tables up,   25
And quench the fire, the room is grown too hot.
Ah, sirrah, this unlook'd-for sport comes well.
Nay, sit, nay, sit, good cousin Capulet;
For you and I are past our dancing days:
How long is't now since last yourself and I   30
Were in a mask?

Second Capulet

> By'r Lady, thirty years.

Capulet

What, man! 'tis not so much, 'tis not so much:
'Tis since the nuptial of Lucentio,
Come Pentecost as quickly as it will,   35
Some five and twenty years; and then we mask'd.

Second Capulet

'Tis more, 'tis more: his son is elder, sir;
His son is thirty.

40 **ward** minor.

54 **should** must.
55 **slave** base fellow.
56 **antic face** grotesque mask.
57 **solemnity** festivity.

Capulet

                    Will you tell me that?
    His son was but a ward two years ago.   40

Romeo
    [*To a Servingman*]   What lady's that, which doth
            enrich the hand
    Of yonder knight?

Servingman
    I know not, sir.

Romeo
    O, she doth teach the torches to burn bright!
    It seems she hangs upon the cheek of night   45
    Like a rich jewel in an Ethiop's ear;
    Beauty too rich for use, for earth too dear!
    So shows a snowy dove trooping with crows,
    As yonder lady o'er her fellows shows.
    The measure done, I'll watch her place of stand,   50
    And, touching hers, make blessed my rude hand.
    Did my heart love till now? forswear it, sight!
    For I ne'er saw true beauty till this night.

Tyball
    This, by his voice, should be a Montague.
    Fetch me my rapier, boy. What dares the slave   55
    Come hither, cover'd with an antic face,
    To fleer and scorn at our solemnity?
    Now, by the stock and honor of my kin,
    To strike him dead I hold it not a sin.

Capulet
    Why, how now, kinsman! wherefore storm you so?   60

Tybalt
    Uncle, this is a Montague, our foe;
    A villain, that is hither come in spite,
    To scorn at our solemnity this night.

Capulet
    Young Romeo is it?

66 **Content thee**   calm yourself.
67 **portly**   dignified.

75 **ill-beseeming semblance**   unbecoming appearance.

79 **goodman boy**   an address indicating inferiority in both rank and age.
   go to   get out.
81 **God shall mend my soul**   exclamation of impatience.
83 **set cock-a-hoop**   be utterly reckless.

87 **what**   what I'm doing.

89 **princox**   conceited youngster.

92 **Patience perforce**   enforced self-restraint.
93 **different greeting**   hostile encounter.

Tybalt
                              'Tis he, that villain Romeo.   65

Capulet
Content thee, gentle coz, let him alone,
He bears him like a portly gentleman;
And, to say truth, Verona brags of him
To be a virtuous and well-govern'd youth:
I would not for the wealth of all this town   70
Here in my house do him disparagement:
Therefore be patient, take no note of him:
It is my will, the which if thou respect,
Show a fair presence and put off these frowns,
An ill-beseeming semblance for a feast.   75

Tybalt
It fits, when such a villain is a guest:
I'll not endure him.

Capulet
                    He shall be endur'd:
What, goodman boy! I say, he shall: go to;
Am I the master here, or you? go to.   80
You'll not endure him! God shall mend my soul,
You'll make a mutiny among my guests!
You will set cock-a-hoop! you'll be the man!

Tybalt
Why, uncle, 'tis a shame.

Capulet
                        Go to, go to;   85
You are a saucy boy: is't so, indeed?
This trick may chance to scathe you, I know what:
You must contrary me! marry, 'tis time.
Well said, my hearts! You are a princox; go:
Be quiet, or—More light, more light! For shame!   90
I'll make you quiet. What, cheerly, my hearts!

Tybalt
Patience perforce with willful choler meeting
Makes my flesh tremble in their different greeting.

First 14 lines of R and J's covo create a sonet

97 shrine refers to Juliet's hand.

103 palmers pilgrims to the Holy Land.

108 move initiate action.

109 effect fulfillment.

I will withdraw: but this intrusion shall,
Now seeming sweet, convert to bitterest gall.   95

[*Exit.*

Romeo

[*To Juliet*]   If I profane with my unworthiest hand
 This holy shrine, the gentle fine is this,
My lips, two blushing pilgrims, ready stand
 To smooth that rough touch with a tender kiss.

Juliet

Good pilgrim, you do wrong your hand too much,   100
 Which mannerly devotion shows in this;
For saints have hands that pilgrims' hands do touch,
 And palm to palm is holy palmers' kiss.

Romeo

Have not saints lips, and holy palmers too?

Juliet

Aye, pilgrim, lips that they must use in prayer.   105

Romeo

O, then, dear saint, let lips do what hands do;
They pray, grant thou, lest faith turn to despair.

Juliet

Saints do not move, though grant for prayers' sake.

Romeo

Then move not, while my prayer's effect I take.
Thus from my lips by thine my sin is purg'd.   110

[*Kissing her.*

Juliet

Then have my lips the sin that they have took.

Romeo

Sin from my lips? O trespass sweetly urg'd!
Give me my sin again.

Juliet

     You kiss by the book.

Nurse

Madam, your mother craves a word with you.   115

120 **withal**   with.

122 **the chinks**   plenty of money.

124 **dear**   (1) expensive; (2) grievous.

128 **foolish**   humble.
    towards   in preparation.

132 **fay**   faith.

Romeo
  What is her mother?

Nurse
                    Marry, bachelor,
  Her mother is the lady of the house,
  And a good lady, and a wise and virtuous:
  I nurs'd her daughter, that you talk'd withal;   120
  I tell you, he that can lay hold of her
  Shall have the chinks.

Romeo
                  Is she a Capulet?
  O dear account! my life is my foe's debt.

Benvolio
  Away, be gone; the sport is at the best.   125

Romeo
  Aye, so I fear; the more is my unrest.

Capulet
  Nay, gentlemen, prepare not to be gone;
  We have a trifling foolish banquet towards.
  Is it e'en so? why, then, I thank you all;
  I thank you, honest gentlemen; good night.   130
  More torches here! Come on then, let's to bed.
  Ah, sirrah, by my fay, it waxes late:
  I'll to my rest.
             [Exeunt all but Juliet and Nurse.

Juliet
  Come hither, nurse. What is yond gentleman?

Nurse
  The son and heir of old Tiberio.   135

Juliet
  What's he that now is going out of door?

Nurse
  Marry, that, I think, be young Petruchio.

Juliet
  What's he that follows there, that would not dance?

146 **Prodigious**   ill-omened.

151 **Anon**   right away.

2 **gapes**   is eager.
3 **fair**   lovely lady.

Nurse
I know not.

Juliet
Go ask his name. If he be married,   140
My grave is like to be my wedding bed.

Nurse
His name is Romeo, and a Montague,
The only son of your great enemy.

Juliet
My only love, sprung from my only hate!
Too early seen unknown, and known too late!   145
Prodigious birth of love it is to me,
That I must love a loathed enemy.

Nurse
What's this? what's this?

Juliet
          A rhyme I learn'd even now
Of one I danced withal.   150
               [*One calls within, "Juliet."*

Nurse
          Anon, anon!
Come, let's away; the strangers all are gone.
               [*Exeunt.*

ACT II

Prologue
~~~~~~~~

Enter Chorus.

Chorus
Now old desire doth in his deathbed lie,
  And young affection gapes to be his heir;
That fair for which love groan'd for and would die,
  With tender Juliet match'd, is now not fair.

Now Romeo is belov'd and loves again,   5
   Alike bewitched by the charm of looks,
But to his foe suppos'd he must complain,
   And she steal love's sweet bait from fearful hooks:
Being held a foe, he may not have access
   To breathe such vows as lovers use to swear;   10
And she as much in love, her means much less
   To meet her new beloved any where:
But passion lends them power, time means, to meet,
Temp'ring extremities with extreme sweet.

                                       [*Exit.*

Scene 1. *A lane by the wall of Capulet's orchard*

Enter Romeo, alone.

Romeo
   Can I go forward when my heart is here?
   Turn back, dull earth, and find thy center out.
      [*He climbs the wall, and leaps down within it.*

   Enter Benvolio with Mercutio.

Benvolio
   Romeo! my cousin Romeo!
Mercutio
                       He is wise;
   And, on my life, hath stol'n him home to bed.   5
Benvolio
   He ran this way, and leap'd this orchard wall;
   Call, good Mercutio.
Mercutio
               Nay, I'll conjure too.
   Romeo! humors! madman! passion! lover!

14 **purblind** totally blind.

16 **King Cophetua** according to an old ballad, Cupid wounded King Cophetua and thereby caused him to marry a beggar maid.

18 **dead** playing dead.

29 **were** would be.
30 **fair** proper.
   honest honorable.

33 **consorted** associated.
   humorous damp.

36 **medlar** fruit resembling a small, brown apple.

41 **truckle-bed** trundle bed.

Appear thou in the likeness of a sigh: 10
Speak but one rhyme, and I am satisfied;
Cry but "aye me!" pronounce but "love" and "dove";
Speak to my gossip Venus one fair word,
One nickname for her purblind son and heir,
Young Adam Cupid, he that shot so trim   15
When King Cophetua loved the beggar maid!
He heareth not, he stirreth not, he moveth not;
The ape is dead, and I must conjure him.
I conjure thee by Rosaline's bright eyes,
By her high forehead and her scarlet lip,   20
By her fine foot, straight leg and quivering thigh,
And the demesnes that there adjacent lie,
That in thy likeness thou appear to us!

Benvolio
An if he hear thee, thou wilt anger him.

Mercutio
This cannot anger him: 'twould anger him   25
To raise a spirit in his mistress' circle
Of some strange nature, letting it there stand
Till she had laid it and conjured it down;
That were some spite: my invocation
Is fair and honest, and in his mistress' name   30
I conjure only but to raise up him.

Benvolio
Come, he hath hid himself among these trees,
To be consorted with the humorous night:
Blind is his love, and best befits the dark.

Mercutio
If love be blind, love cannot hit the mark.   35
Now will he sit under a medlar tree,
And wish his mistress were that kind of fruit
As maids call medlars when they laugh alone.
O, Romeo, that she were, O, that she were
An open et cetera, thou a pop'rin pear!   40
Romeo, good night: I'll to my truckle-bed;

42 **field-bed**   bare earth.

2 **soft!**   hush.

8 **vestal livery**   virginal uniform.

17 **spheres**   orbits.

This field-bed is too cold for me to sleep:
Come, shall we go?

Benvolio
                    Go then, for 'tis in vain
To seek him here that means not to be found.   45

                                        [*Exeunt.*

Scene 2. Capulet's orchard

Enter Romeo.

Romeo
He jests at scars that never felt a wound.
                    [*Juliet appears above at a window.*
But, soft! what light through yonder window breaks?
It is the east, and Juliet is the sun!
Arise, fair sun, and kill the envious moon,
Who is already sick and pale with grief,   5
That thou her maid are far more fair than she:
Be not her maid, since she is envious;
Her vestal livery is but sick and green,
And none but fools do wear it; cast it off.
It is my lady; O, it is my love!   10
O, that she knew she were!
She speaks, yet she says nothing: what of that?
Her eye discourses, I will answer it.
I am too bold, 'tis not to me she speaks:
Two of the fairest stars in all the heaven,   15
Having some business, do entreat her eyes
To twinkle in their spheres till they return.
What if her eyes were there, they in her head?
The brightness of her cheek would shame those stars,
As daylight doth a lamp; her eyes in heaven   20
Would through the airy region stream so bright
That birds would sing and think it were not night.

35 **wherefore**   why.

41 **though not**   even if you were not.

48 **owes**   owns.

See, how she leans her cheek upon her hand!
O, that I were a glove upon that hand,
That I might touch that cheek!   25

Juliet

Aye me!

Romeo

She speaks:

O, speak again, bright angel! for thou art
As glorious to this night, being o'er my head,
As is a winged messenger of heaven   30
Unto the white-upturned wond'ring eyes
Of mortals that fall back to gaze on him
When he bestrides the lazy-pacing clouds
And sails upon the bosom of the air.

Juliet

O Romeo, Romeo! wherefore art thou Romeo?   35
Deny thy father and refuse thy name;
Or, if thou wilt not, be but sworn my love,
And I'll no longer be a Capulet.

Romeo

[*Aside*] Shall I hear more, or shall I speak at this?

Juliet

'Tis but thy name that is my enemy;   40
Thou art thyself, though not a Montague.
What's Montague? it is nor hand, nor foot,
Nor arm, nor face, nor any other part
Belonging to a man. O, be some other name!
What's in a name? that which we call a rose   45
By any other name would smell as sweet;
So Romeo would, were he not Romeo call'd,
Retain that dear perfection which he owes
Without that title. Romeo, doff thy name,
And for thy name, which is no part of thee,   50
Take all myself.

Romeo

I take thee at thy word:

56 **counsel** secret thoughts.

61 **written** in writing.

70 **o'erperch** fly over.

73 **let** hindrance.

77 **proof** armored.

Call me but love, and I'll be new baptiz'd;
Henceforth I never will be Romeo.

Juliet

What man art thou, that, thus bescreen'd in night,   55
So stumblest on my counsel?

Romeo

By a name
I know not how to tell thee who I am:
My name, dear saint, is hateful to myself,
Because it is an enemy to thee;   60
Had I it written, I would tear the word.

Juliet

My ears have yet not drunk a hundred words
Of thy tongue's uttering, yet I know the sound:
Art thou not Romeo, and a Montague?

Romeo

Neither, fair maid, if either thee dislike.   65

Juliet

How cam'st thou hither, tell me, and wherefore?
The orchard walls are high and hard to climb,
And the place death, considering who thou art,
If any of my kinsmen find thee here.

Romeo

With love's light wings did I o'erperch these walls,   70
For stony limits cannot hold love out:
And what love can do, that dares love attempt;
Therefore thy kinsmen are no let to me.

Juliet

If they do see thee, they will murder thee.

Romeo

Alack, there lies more peril in thine eye   75
Than twenty of their swords: look thou but sweet,
And I am proof against their enmity.

Juliet

I would not for the world they saw thee here.

80 **but**   unless.

82 **prorogued**   postponed.

92 **Fain**   gladly.
   dwell on form   linger over formal niceties.
93 **compliment**   conventions.

102 **fond**   foolishly affectionate.
103 **light**   immodest.

105 **strange**   reserved.

110 **discovered**   revealed.

Romeo
> I have night's cloak to hide me from their eyes;
> And but thou love me, let them find me here: 80
> My life were better ended by their hate,
> Than death prorogued, wanting of thy love.

Juliet
> By whose direction found'st thou out this place?

Romeo
> By love, that first did prompt me to inquire;
> He lent me counsel, and I lent him eyes.   85
> I am no pilot; yet, wert thou as far
> As that vast shore wash'd with the farthest sea,
> I would adventure for such merchandise.

Juliet
> Thou know'st the mask of night is on my face,
> Else would a maiden blush bepaint my cheek   90
> For that which thou hast heard me speak tonight.
> Fain would I dwell on form, fain, fain deny
> What I have spoke: but farewell compliment!
> Dost thou love me? I know thou wilt say "Aye,"
> And I will take thy word: yet, if thou swear'st,   95
> Thou mayst prove false: at lovers' perjuries,
> They say, Jove laughs. O gentle Romeo,
> If thou dost love, pronounce it faithfully:
> Or if thou think'st I am too quickly won,
> I'll frown and be perverse and say thee nay,   100
> So thou wilt woo; but else, not for the world.
> In truth, fair Montague, I am too fond;
> And therefore thou mayst think my 'havior light:
> But trust me, gentleman, I'll prove more true
> Than those that have more cunning to be strange.   105
> I should have been more strange, I must confess,
> But that thou overheard'st, ere I was ware,
> My true love's passion: therefore pardon me,
> And not impute this yielding to light love,
> Which the dark night hath so discovered.   110

114 **circled orb**   sphere of the moon.

123 **contract**   exchange of vows.
124 **unadvis'd**   heedless, ill-considered.

Romeo

>   Lady, by yonder blessed moon I swear,
>   That tips with silver all these fruit-tree tops—

Juliet

>   O, swear not by the moon, th'inconstant moon,
>   That monthly changes in her circled orb,
>   Lest that thy love prove likewise variable.   115

Romeo

>   What shall I swear by?

Juliet

>   Do not swear at all;
>   Or, if thou wilt, swear by thy gracious self,
>   Which is the god of my idolatry,
>   And I'll believe thee.   120

Romeo

>   If my heart's dear love—

Juliet

>   Well, do not swear: although I joy in thee,
>   I have no joy of this contract tonight:
>   It is too rash, too unadvis'd, too sudden,
>   Too like the lightning, which doth cease to be   125
>   Ere one can say "It lightens." Sweet, good night!
>   This bud of love, by summer's ripening breath,
>   May prove a beauteous flower when next we meet.
>   Good night, good night! as sweet repose and rest
>   Come to thy heart as that within my breast!   130

Romeo

>   O, wilt thou leave me so unsatisfied?

Juliet

>   What satisfaction canst thou have tonight?

Romeo

>   The exchange of thy love's faithful vow for mine.

Juliet

>   I gave thee mine before thou didst request it:
>   And yet I would it were to give again.   135

137 **frank**   generous.

149 **bent**   intention.

151 **procure**   arrange for.

159 **By and by**   at once.

Romeo
> Wouldst thou withdraw it? for what purpose, love?

Juliet
> But to be frank, and give it thee again.
> And yet I wish but for the thing I have:
> My bounty is as boundless as the sea,
> My love as deep; the more I give to thee, 140
> The more I have, for both are infinite.
> I hear some noise within; dear love, adieu!
>   [*Nurse calls within.*
> Anon, good nurse! Sweet Montague, be true.
> Stay but a little, I will come again.
>   [*Exit.*

Romeo
> O blessed, blessed night! I am afeard, 145
> Being in night, all this is but a dream,
> Too flattering-sweet to be substantial.

>   *Reenter Juliet, above.*

Juliet
> Three words, dear Romeo, and good night indeed.
> If that thy bent of love be honorable,
> Thy purpose marriage, send me word tomorrow, 150
> By one that I'll procure to come to thee,
> Where and what time thou wilt perform the rite,
> And all my fortunes at thy foot I'll lay,
> And follow thee my lord throughout the world.

Nurse
> [*Within*]   Madam! 155

Juliet
> I come, anon.—But if thou mean'st not well,
> I do beseech thee—

Nurse
> [*Within*]   Madam!

Juliet
>   By and by, I come:—

168 tassel-gentle   male falcon.

To cease thy suit, and leave me to my grief: 160
Tomorrow will I send.

Romeo

So thrive my soul—

Juliet

A thousand times good night!

[*Exit.*

Romeo

A thousand times the worse, to want thy light.
Love goes toward love, as schoolboys from their books, 165
But love from love, toward school with heavy looks.

[*Retiring slowly.*

Reenter Juliet, above.

Juliet

Hist! Romeo, hist!—O, for a falc'ner's voice,
To lure this tassel-gentle back again!
Bondage is hoarse, and may not speak aloud;
Else would I tear the cave where Echo lies, 170
And make her airy tongue more hoarse than mine,
With repetition of my Romeo's name.
Romeo!

Romeo

It is my soul that calls upon my name:
How silver-sweet sound lovers' tongues by night, 175
Like softest music to attending ears!

Juliet

Romeo!

Romeo

My dear?

Juliet

At what o'clock tomorrow
Shall I send to thee? 180

Romeo

At the hour of nine.

185 **still**   always.

190 **wanton**   capricious child.

192 **gyves**   bonds, fetters.

202 **ghostly**   spiritual.
203 **dear hap**   good fortune.

Juliet

    I will not fail: 'tis twenty years till then.
    I have forgot why I did call thee back.

Romeo

    Let me stand here till thou remember it.

Juliet

    I shall forget, to have thee still stand there,   185
    Remembering how I love thy company.

Romeo

    And I'll still stay, to have thee still forget,
    Forgetting any other home but this.

Juliet

    'Tis almost morning; I would have thee gone:
    And yet no farther than a wanton's bird,   190
    Who lets it hop a little from her hand,
    Like a poor prisoner in his twisted gyves,
    And with a silk thread plucks it back again,
    So loving-jealous of his liberty.

Romeo

    I would I were thy bird.   195

Juliet

                   Sweet, so would I:
    Yet I should kill thee with much cherishing.
    Good night, good night! parting is such sweet sorrow
    That I shall say good night till it be morrow.

                                        [*Exit.*

Romeo

    Sleep dwell upon thine eyes, peace in thy breast!   200
    Would I were sleep and peace, so sweet to rest!
    Hence will I to my ghostly father's cell,
    His help to crave, and my dear hap to tell.

                                        [*Exit.*

4 **Titan** the sun god.
wheels that is, of the sun's chariot.
5 **advance** raise.
7 **osier cage** wicker basket.

15 **mickle** great.
grace virtue, effectiveness.

19 **strain'd** perverted.

25 **that part** its odor.

28 **will** lust.

30 **canker** canker worm, devourer of flowers.

Scene 3. *Friar Laurence's cell*

Enter Friar Laurence, with a basket.

Friar Laurence
  The gray-ey'd morn smiles on the frowning night,
  Chequering the eastern clouds with streaks of light;
  And flecked darkness like a drunkard reels
  From forth day's path and Titan's fiery wheels:
  Now, ere the sun advance his burning eye,   5
  The day to cheer and night's dank dew to dry,
  I must up-fill this osier cage of ours
  With baleful weeds and precious-juiced flowers.
  The earth that's nature's mother is her tomb;
  What is her burying grave, that is her womb: 10
  And from her womb children of divers kind
  We sucking on her natural bosom find,
  Many for many virtues excellent,
  None but for some, and yet all different.
  O, mickle is the pow'rful grace that lies   15
  In herbs, plants, stones, and their true qualities:
  For nought so vile that on the earth doth live,
  But to the earth some special good doth give;
  Nor aught so good, but, strain'd from that fair use,
  Revolts from true birth, stumbling on abuse: 20
  Virtue itself turns vice, being misapplied,
  And vice sometime's by action dignified.
  Within the infant rind of this small flower
  Poison hath residence, and medicine power:
  For this, being smelt, with that part cheers each part,   25
  Being tasted, slays all senses with the heart.
  Two such opposed kings encamp them still
  In man as well as herbs, grace and rude will;
  And where the worser is predominant,
  Full soon the canker death eats up that plant.   30

32 **Benedicite!** God bless you.

53 **physic** healing power.
55 **intercession** petition.
   steads benefits.
56 **homely** simple.
   drift narrative.
57 **shrift** absolution.

Enter Romeo.

Romeo
Good morrow, father.

Friar Laurence
                  Benedicite!
What early tongue so sweet saluteth me?
Young son, it argues a distemper'd head
So soon to bid good morrow to thy bed: 35
Care keeps his watch in every old man's eye,
And where care lodges, sleep will never lie;
But where unbruised youth with unstuff'd brain
Doth couch his limbs, there golden sleep doth reign:
Therefore thy earliness doth me assure   40
Thou art uprous'd by some distemp'rature;
Or if not so, then here I hit it right,
Our Romeo hath not been in bed tonight.

Romeo
That last is true; the sweeter rest was mine.

Friar Laurence
God pardon sin! wast thou with Rosaline?   45

Romeo
With Rosaline, my ghostly father? no;
I have forgot that name and that name's woe.

Friar Laurence
That's my good son: but where hast thou been then?

Romeo
I'll tell thee ere thou ask it me again.
I have been feasting with mine enemy;   50
Where on a sudden one hath wounded me,
That's by me wounded: both our remedies
Within thy help and holy physic lies:
I bear no hatred, blessed man, for, lo,
My intercession likewise steads my foe.   55

Friar Laurence
Be plain, good son, and homely in thy drift;
Riddling confession finds but riddling shrift.

61 **all combin'd**   united spiritually.

80 **sentence**   maxim.

Romeo

Then plainly know my heart's dear love is set
On the fair daughter of rich Capulet:
As mine on hers, so hers is set on mine;   60
And all combin'd, save what thou must combine
By holy marriage: when, and where, and how
We met, we woo'd and made exchange of vow,
I'll tell thee as we pass; but this I pray,
That thou consent to marry us today.   65

Friar Laurence

Holy Saint Francis, what a change is here!
Is Rosaline, that thou didst love so dear,
So soon forsaken? young men's love then lies
Not truly in their hearts, but in their eyes.
Jesu Maria, what a deal of brine   70
Hath wash'd thy sallow cheeks for Rosaline!
How much salt water thrown away in waste,
To season love, that of it doth not taste!
The sun not yet thy sighs from heaven clears,
Thy old groans ring yet in mine ancient ears;   75
Lo, here upon thy cheek the stain doth sit
Of an old tear that is not wash'd off yet:
If e'er thou wast thyself and these woes thine,
Thou and these woes were all for Rosaline:
And art thou chang'd? pronounce this sentence then: 80
Women may fall when there's no strength in men.

Romeo

Thou chid'st me oft for loving Rosaline.

Friar Laurence

For doting, not for loving, pupil mine.

Romeo

And bad'st me bury love.

Friar Laurence

                              Not in a grave,   85
To lay one in, another out to have.

88 **grace**   favor.

91 **read**   recite.

93 **In one respect**   for one reason.

96 **stand**   insist.

2 **tonight**   last night.

Romeo
    I pray thee, chide not: she whom I love now
    Doth grace for grace and love for love allow;
    The other did not so.

Friar Laurence
                    O, she knew well   90
    Thy love did read by rote and could not spell.
    But come, young waverer, come, go with me,
    In one respect I'll thy assistant be;
    For this alliance may so happy prove,
    To turn your households' rancor to pure love.   95

Romeo
    O, let us hence; I stand on sudden haste.

Friar Laurence
    Wisely and slow: they stumble that run fast.

                                    [*Exeunt.*

Scene 4. A street
━━━━━━━━━━━

Enter Benvolio and Mercutio.

Mercutio
    Where the devil should this Romeo be?
    Came he not home tonight?

Benvolio
    Not to his father's; I spoke with his man.

Mercutio
    Ah, that same pale hard-hearted wench, that Rosaline,
    Torments him so that he will sure run mad.   5

Benvolio
    Tybalt, the kinsman to old Capulet,
    Hath sent a letter to his father's house.

Mercutio
    A challenge, on my life.

9 **answer** accept.

15–16 **blind bow-boy** Cupid.
16 **butt-shaft** practice arrow.

19 **prince of cats** play on Tybalt's name; Tybert is the name given to the cat in the animal story *Reynard the Fox*.
20 **compliments** courteous formalities.
21 **pricksong** written music.
22 **minim rest** short pause (in music).
24 **very first house** finest fencing school.
25 **cause** cause for dueling.
25–26 **passado; punto reverso; hai** fencing strokes.

28 **The pox of** the plague take.
antic absurd.　**fantasticoes** affected persons.
29 **new tuners of accents** users of fashionable new phrases.
30 **tall** brave.
32 **flies** parasites.

Benvolio
Romeo will answer it.

Mercutio
Any man that can write may answer a letter.   10

Benvolio
Nay, he will answer the letter's master, how he dares,
being dared.

Mercutio
Alas, poor Romeo, he is already dead! stabbed with a
white wench's black eye; shot through the ear with a
love song; the very pin of his heart cleft with the blind   15
bow-boy's butt-shaft: and is he a man to encounter
Tybalt?

Benvolio
Why, what is Tybalt?

Mercutio
More than prince of cats, I can tell you. O, he's the
courageous captain of compliments. He fights as you   20
sing pricksong, keeps time, distance and proportion;
rest me his minim rest, one, two, and the third in your
bosom: the very butcher of a silk button, a duelist, a
duelist; a gentleman of the very first house, of the first
and second cause: ah, the immortal passado! the punto   25
reverso! the hai!

Benvolio
The what?

Mercutio
The pox of such antic, lisping, affecting fantasticoes;
these new tuners of accents! "By Jesu, a very good
blade! a very tall man! a very good whore!" Why, is   30
not this a lamentable thing, grandsire, that we should
be thus afflicted with these strange flies, these fashion-
mongers, these perdonami's, who stand so much on
the new form that they cannot sit at ease on the old
bench? O, their bones, their bones!   35

38 **numbers**   verses.

39 **Petrarch**   Italian poet whose love sonnets became models for later poets.

Laura   Petrarch's beloved.

41–42 **Dido, Cleopatra, Helen, Hero, Thisbe**   famous lovers of myth and history.

42 **hildings**   worthless creatures.

44 **slop**   baggy breeches.

Enter Romeo.

Benvolio
Here comes Romeo, here comes Romeo.

Mercutio
Without his roe, like a dried herring: O flesh, flesh,
how art thou fishified! Now is he for the numbers that
Petrarch flowed in: Laura to his lady was but a kitchen
wench; marry, she had a better love to berhyme her;   40
Dido, a dowdy; Cleopatra, a gipsy; Helen and Hero,
hildings and harlots; Thisbe, a gray eye or so, but not
to the purpose. Signior Romeo, bon jour! there's a
French salutation to your French slop. You gave us the
counterfeit fairly last night.   45

Romeo
Good morrow to you both. What counterfeit did I give
you?

Mercutio
The slip, sir, the slip; can you not conceive?

Romeo
Pardon, good Mercutio, my business was great; and
in such a case as mine a man may strain courtesy.   50

Mercutio
That's as much as to say, such a case as yours con-
strains a man to bow in the hams.

Romeo
Meaning, to curtsy.

Mercutio
Thou hast most kindly hit it.

Romeo
A most courteous exposition.   55

Mercutio
Nay, I am the very pink of courtesy.

Romeo
Pink for flower.

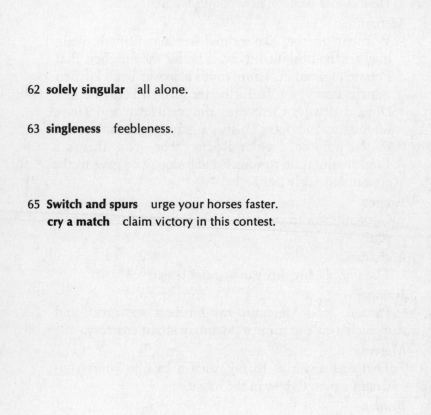

62 **solely singular**   all alone.

63 **singleness**   feebleness.

65 **Switch and spurs**   urge your horses faster.
cry a match   claim victory in this contest.

74 **sweeting**   a variety of apple.

77 **cheveril**   an elastic leather.

Mercutio
Right.

Romeo
Why, then is my pump well flowered.

Mercutio
Well said: follow me this jest now, till thou hast worn   60
out thy pump, that, when the single sole of it is worn,
the jest may remain, after the wearing, solely singular.

Romeo
O single-sol'd jest, solely singular for the singleness!

Mercutio
Come between us, good Benvolio; my wits faint.

Romeo
Switch and spurs, switch and spurs; or I'll cry a match.   65

Mercutio
Nay, if thy wits run the wild-goose chase, I have done;
for thou hast more of the wild goose in one of thy wits
than, I am sure, I have in my whole five: was I with
you there for the goose?

Romeo
Thou wast never with me for anything when thou wast   70
not there for the goose.

Mercutio
I will bite thee by the ear for that jest.

Romeo
Nay, good goose, bite not.

Mercutio
Thy wit is a very bitter sweeting; it is a most sharp
sauce.   75

Romeo
And is it not well serv'd in to a sweet goose?

Mercutio
O, here's a wit of cheveril, that stretches from an inch
narrow to an ell broad!

80 **broad**   evident.

84 **natural**   idiot.

92 **goodly gear**   handsome merchandise, matters for jest.

Romeo

I stretch it out for that word "broad," which added to
the goose, proves thee far and wide a broad goose.   80

Mercutio

Why, is not this better now than groaning for love?
now art thou sociable, now art thou Romeo; now art
thou what thou art, by art as well as by nature: for this
driveling love is like a great natural, that runs lolling
up and down to hide his bauble in a hole.   85

Benvolio

Stop there, stop there.

Mercutio

Thou desirest me to stop in my tale against the hair.

Benvolio

Thou wouldst else have made thy tale large.

Mercutio

O, thou art deceiv'd; I would have made it short: for
I was come to the whole depth of my tale, and meant   90
indeed to occupy the argument no longer.

Romeo

Here's goodly gear!

    Enter Nurse and Peter.

Mercutio

A sail, a sail!

Benvolio

Two, two; a shirt and a smock.

Nurse

Peter!   95

Peter

Anon.

Nurse

My fan, Peter.

Mercutio

Good Peter, to hide her face; for her fan's the fairer
of the two.

100 **God ye good morrow**   God give you good morning.

101 **God ye good den**   God give you good evening.

105 **Out upon you!**   expression of indignation.

107 **By my troth**   truly.

117 **confidence**   conference.

118 **indite**   deliberately misused for invite.

119 **bawd**   go-between.
So ho!   hunter's cry upon sighting game.

Nurse
God ye good morrow, gentlemen.   100

Mercutio
God ye good den, fair gentlewoman.

Nurse
Is it good den?

Mercutio
'Tis no less, I tell you; for the bawdy hand of the dial
is now upon the prick of noon.

Nurse
Out upon you! what a man are you!   105

Romeo
One, gentlewoman, that God hath made himself to mar.

Nurse
By my troth, it is well said; "For himself to mar,"
quoth 'a? Gentlemen, can any of you tell me where I
may find the young Romeo?

Romeo
I can tell you; but young Romeo will be older when   110
you have found him than he was when you sought
him: I am the youngest of that name, for fault of a
worse.

Nurse
You say well.

Mercutio
Yea, is the worst well? very well took, i' faith; wisely,   115
wisely.

Nurse
If you be he, sir, I desire some confidence with you.

Benvolio
She will indite him to some supper.

Mercutio
A bawd, a bawd, a bawd! So ho!

Romeo
What hast thou found?   120

134 **merchant**   fellow.
135 **ropery**   rascally talk (which could lead to the gallows).

137 **stand to**   live up to.

140 **Jacks**   rascals.
141 **Scurvy**   contemptible.
142 **flirt-gills**   flirty wenches.
142–143 **skains-mates**   cutthroats.

Mercutio

No hare, sir; unless a hare, sir, in a lenten pie, that is
something stale and hoar ere it be spent.

[*Sings*]

An old hare hoar,
And an old hare hoar,
Is very good meat in lent:　　　　　　　　　　125
But a hare that is hoar,
It soo much for a score,
When it hoars ere it be spent.

Romeo, will you come to your father's? we'll to dinner
thither.　　　　　　　　　　　　　　　　　　130

Romeo

I will follow you.

Mercutio

Farewell, ancient lady; farewell, [*Singing*] "lady,
lady, lady."

　　　　　　　　　[*Exeunt Mercutio and Benvolio.*

Nurse

Marry, farewell! I pray you, sir, what saucy merchant
was this, that was so full of his ropery?　　　　135

Romeo

A gentleman, nurse, that loves to hear himself talk,
and will speak more in a minute than he will stand to
in a month.

Nurse

An 'a speak any thing against me, I'll take him down,
an 'a were lustier than he is, and twenty such Jacks;　140
and if I cannot, I'll find those that shall. Scurvy knave.
I am none of his flirt-gills; I am none of his skains-
mates. [*Turning to Peter*]　And thou must stand by
too, and suffer every knave to use me at his pleasure?

Peter

I saw no man use you at his pleasure; if I had, my　145
weapon should quickly have been out, I warrant you:

154 **were** would be.

159 **commend me** give my respectful greetings.
protest declare.

163 **mark** heed.

167 **shrift** absolution.

169 **shriv'd** absolved.

I dare draw as soon as another man, if I see occasion in
a good quarrel and the law on my side.

Nurse

Now, afore God, I am so vexed that every part about
me quivers. Scurvy knave! Pray you, sir, a word: and as 150
I told you, my young lady bade me inquire you out;
what she bade me say, I will keep to myself: but first let
me tell ye, if ye should lead her into a fool's paradise,
as they say, it were a very gross kind of behavior, as
they say: for the gentlewoman is young, and therefore, 155
if you should deal double with her, truly it were an ill
thing to be offered to any gentlewoman, and very weak
dealing.

Romeo

Nurse, commend me to thy lady and mistress. I protest
unto thee— 160

Nurse

Good heart, and, i' faith, I will tell her as much: Lord,
Lord, she will be a joyful woman.

Romeo

What wilt thou tell her, nurse? thou dost not mark me.

Nurse

I will tell her, sir, that you do protest; which, as I take
it, is a gentlemanlike offer. 165

Romeo

Bid her devise
Some means to come to shrift this afternoon;
And there she shall at Friar Laurence' cell
Be shriv'd and married. Here is for thy pains.

Nurse

No, truly, sir; not a penny. 170

Romeo

Go to; I say you shall.

Nurse

This afternoon, sir? well, she shall be there.

175 **tackled stair** rope ladder.
176 **topgallant** pinnacle.

178 **quit** reward.

182 **secret** trustworthy.

187 **fain** gladly.
187–188 **lay knife aboard** like a pirate, take what he desires for his own.
188 **lieve** willingly.
190 **properer** handsomer.
191 **clout** rag.
192 **versal world** universe.

195 **dog's name** because the leter r sounds like a dog growling.

Romeo

And stay, good nurse, behind the abbey wall:
Within this hour my man shall be with thee,
And bring thee cords made like a tackled stair;   175
Which to the high topgallant of my joy
Must be my convoy in the secret night.
Farewell; be trusty, and I'll quit thy pains:
Farewell; commend me to thy mistress.

Nurse

Now God in heaven bless thee! Hark you, sir.   180

Romeo

What say'st thou, my dear nurse?

Nurse

Is your man secret? Did you ne'er hear say,
Two may keep counsel, putting one away?

Romeo

I warrant thee, my man's as true as steel.

Nurse

Well, sir; my mistress is the sweetest lady—Lord,   185
Lord! when 'twas a little prating thing—O, there is a
nobleman in town, one Paris, that would fain lay knife
aboard; but she, good soul, had as lieve see a toad, a
very toad, as see him. I anger her sometimes, and tell
her that Paris is the properer man; but, I'll warrant   190
you, when I say so, she looks as pale as any clout in the
versal world. Doth not rosemary and Romeo begin
both with a letter?

Romeo

Aye, nurse; what of that? both with an R.

Nurse

Ah, mocker! that's the dog's name; R is for the—No;   195
I know it begins with some other letter—and she hath
the prettiest sententious of it, of you and rosemary,
that it would do you good to hear it.

Romeo

Commend me to thy lady.

203 **apace**   quickly.

7 **nimble-pinion'd**   swift-winged.

12 **affections**   emotional capacity.

16 **as**   as if

Nurse
     Aye, a thousand times.   200
     [*Exit Romeo.*]   Peter!
Peter
     Anon?
Nurse
     Peter, take my fan, and go before, and apace.
                                              [*Exeunt.*

Scene 5. *Capulet's orchard*

Enter Juliet.

Juliet
     The clock struck nine when I did send the nurse;
     In half an hour she promis'd to return.
     Perchance she cannot meet him: that's not so.
     O, she is lame! love's heralds should be thoughts,
     Which ten times faster glide than the sun's beams,   5
     Driving back shadows over low'ring hills:
     Therefore do nimble-pinion'd doves draw love,
     And therefore hath the wind-swift Cupid wings.
     Now is the sun upon the highmost hill
     Of this day's journey, and from nine till twelve   10
     Is three long hours; yet she is not come.
     Had she affections and warm youthful blood,
     She would be as swift in motion as a ball;
     My words would bandy her to my sweet love,
     And his to me: 15
     But old folks, many feign as they were dead;
     Unwieldy, slow, heavy and pale as lead.

          Enter Nurse, with Peter.

     O God, she comes! O honey nurse, what news?
     Hast thou met with him? Send thy man away.

25 **give me leave** excuse me.
26 **jaunce** rough journey.

36 **stay the circumstance** wait to hear the details.

Nurse

    Peter, stay at the gate.   20

                                  [*Exit Peter.*

Juliet

    Now, good sweet nurse—O Lord, why look'st thou
        sad?

    Though news be sad, yet tell them merrily;

    If good, thou shamest the music of sweet news

    By playing it to me with so sour a face.

Nurse

    I am aweary; give me leave awhile.   25

    Fie, how my bones ache! what a jaunce have I had!

Juliet

    I would thou hadst my bones and I thy news:

    Nay, come, I pray thee, speak; good, good nurse, speak

Nurse

    Jesu, what haste! can you not stay a while?

    Do you not see that I am out of breath?   30

Juliet

    How art thou out of breath, when thou hast breath

    To say to me that thou art out of breath?

    The excuse that thou dost make in this delay

    Is longer than the tale thou dost excuse.

    Is thy news good, or bad? answer to that;   35

    Say either, and I'll stay the circumstance:

    Let me be satisfied, is't good or bad?

Nurse

    Well, you have made a simple choice; you know not

    how to choose a man: Romeo! no, not he; though his

    face be better than any man's, yet his leg excels all   40

    men's; and for a hand, and a foot, and a body, though

    they be not to be talked on, yet they are past compare:

    he is not the flower of courtesy, but, I'll warrant him,

    as gentle as a lamb. Go thy ways, wench; serve God.

    What, have you dined at home?   45

51 **Beshrew** curse.

62 **God's Lady dear** the Virgin Mary.
63 **marry, come up** expression of angry impatience.
 trow declare.

66 **coil** fuss.

69 **hie** hasten.

Juliet

No, no: but all this did I know before.
What says he of our marriage? what of that?

Nurse

Lord, how my head aches! what a head have I!
It beats as it would fall in twenty pieces.
My back o' t' other side,—ah, my back, my back!   50
Beshrew your heart for sending me about,
To catch my death with jauncing up and down!

Juliet

I' faith, I am sorry that thou art not well.
Sweet, sweet, sweet nurse, tell me, what says my love?

Nurse

Your love says, like an honest gentleman, and a cour-   55
teous, and a kind, and a handsome, and, I warrant, a
virtuous—Where is your mother?

Juliet

Where is my mother! why, she is within;
Where should she be? How oddly thou repliest!
"Your love says, like an honest gentleman,   60
'Where is your mother?' "

Nurse

                              O God's Lady dear!
Are you so hot? marry, come up, I trow;
Is this the poultice for my aching bones?
Henceforward do your messages yourself.   65

Juliet

Here's such a coil! come, what says Romeo?

Nurse

Have you got leave to go to shrift today?

Juliet

I have.

Nurse

Then hie you hence to Friar Laurence' cell;
There stays a husband to make you a wife: 70

71 **wanton** uncontrolled.

77 **soon at night** this very night.

3 **what** whatever.
4 **countervail** outweigh.

13 **confounds** destroys.

Now comes the wanton blood up in your cheeks,
They'll be in scarlet straight at any news.
Hie you to church; I must another way,
To fetch a ladder, by the which your love
Must climb a bird's nest soon when it is dark;   75
I am the drudge, and toil in your delight;
But you shall bear the burthen soon at night.
Go; I'll to dinner; hie you to the cell.

Juliet
Hie to high fortune! Honest nurse, farewell.

[*Exeunt.*

Scene 6. *Friar Laurence's cell*

Enter Friar Laurence and Romeo.

Friar Laurence
So smile the heavens upon this holy act
That after-hours with sorrow chide us not!

Romeo
Amen, amen! but come what sorrow can,
It cannot countervail the exchange of joy
That one short minute gives me in her sight: 5
Do thou but close our hands with holy words,
Then love-devouring death do what he dare,
It is enough I may but call her mine.

Friar Laurence
These violent delights have violent ends,
And in their triumph die; like fire and powder   10
Which as they kiss consume: the sweetest honey
Is loathsome in his own deliciousness,
And in the taste confounds the appetite:
Therefore, love moderately; long love doth so;
Too swift arrives as tardy as too slow.   15

18 **gossamer**   cobweb.
19 **wanton**   sportive.
20 **vanity**   earthly.

23 **As much**   the same.

25 **that**   if.
26 **blazon**   proclaim.

30 **Conceit**   understanding.

34 **sum up sum**   add up the total.

Enter Juliet.

Here comes the lady. O, so light a foot
Will ne'er wear out the everlasting flint.
A lover may bestride the gossamer
That idles in the wanton summer air,
And yet not fall; so light is vanity.   20

Juliet
Good even to my ghostly confessor.

Friar Laurence
Romeo shall thank thee, daughter, for us both.

Juliet
As much to him, else is his thanks too much.

Romeo
Ah, Juliet, if the measure of thy joy
Be heap'd like mine, and that thy skill be more   25
To blazon it, then sweeten with thy breath
This neighbor air, and let rich music's tongue
Unfold the imagined happiness that both
Receive in either by this dear encounter.

Juliet
Conceit, more rich in matter than in words,   30
Brags of his substance, not of ornament:
They are but beggars that can count their worth;
But my true love is grown to such excess,
I cannot sum up sum of half my wealth.

Friar Laurence
Come, come with me, and we will make short work;   35
For, by your leaves, you shall not stay alone
Till holy church incorporate two in one.

                                        [*Exeunt.*

8 **by the operation of the second cup**   when he feels the effects of the second drink.

9 **drawer**   waiter.

11 **Jack**   fellow.

12 **moved to be moody**   apt to be angered.

13 **moody to be moved**   angry at being provoked.

ACT III

Scene 1. A *public place*

Enter Mercutio, Benvolio, Page, and Servants.

Benvolio
I pray thee, good Mercutio, let's retire:
The day is hot, the Capulets abroad,
And if we meet, we shall not 'scape a brawl;
For now these hot days is the mad blood stirring.

Mercutio
Thou art like one of those fellows that when he enters   5
the confines of a tavern claps me his sword upon the
table, and says "God send me no need of thee!" and
by the operation of the second cup draws it on the
drawer, when indeed there is no need.

Benvolio
Am I like such a fellow?   10

Mercutio
Come, come, thou art as hot a Jack in thy mood as any
in Italy, and as soon moved to be moody, and as soon
moody to be moved.

Benvolio
And what to?

Mercutio
Nay, an there were two such, we should have none   15
shortly, for one would kill the other. Thou! why, thou
wilt quarrel with a man that hath a hair more, or a
hair less, in his beard than thou hast: thou wilt quarrel

23 **addle** confused.

27 **doublet** jacket.
28 **riband** ribbon.

31 **fee-simple** inheritance, therefore, unconditional owner-
ship.
an hour and a quarter a trifling sum.

42 **consort'st** do associate.

with a man for cracking nuts, having no other reason
but because thou hast hazel eyes; what eye, but such   20
an eye, would spy out such a quarrel? thy head is as
full of quarrels as an egg is full of meat, and yet thy
head hath been beaten as addle as an egg for quarreling: thou hast quarreled with a man for coughing in
the street, because he hath wakened thy dog that hath   25
lain asleep in the sun: didst thou not fall out with a
tailor for wearing his new doublet before Easter? with
another, for tying his new shoes with old riband? and
yet thou wilt tutor me from quarreling!

Benvolio

An I were so apt to quarrel as thou art, any man should   30
buy the fee-simple of my life for an hour and a quarter.

Mercutio

The fee-simple! O simple!

    Enter Tybalt and others.

Benvolio

By my head, here come the Capulets.

Mercutio

By my heel, I care not,

Tybalt

Follow me close, for I will speak to them.   35
Gentlemen, good den: a word with one of you.

Mercutio

And but one word with one of us? couple it with something; make it a word and a blow.

Tybalt

You shall find me apt enough to that, sir, an you will
give me occasion.   40

Mercutio

Could you not take some occasion without giving?

Tybalt

Mercutio, thou consort'st with Romeo.

43 **Consort**   associate; also a company of musicians.

46 **'Zounds**   by God's wounds.

54 **livery**   uniform.
55 **to field**   that is, a dueling field.

58 **villain**   base person.

60 **appertaining**   suitable.

66 **devise**   imagine.

Mercutio
   Consort! what, dost thou make us minstrels? an thou
   make minstrels of us, look to hear nothing but discords: here's my fiddlestick; here's that shall make you   45
   dance. 'Zounds, consort!

Benvolio
   We talk here in the public haunt of men:
   Either withdraw into some private place,
   Or reason coldly of your grievances,
   Or else depart; here all eyes gaze on us.   50

Mercutio
   Men's eyes were made to look, and let them gaze;
   I will not budge for no man's pleasure, I.

      Enter Romeo.

Tybalt
   Well, peace be with you, sir: here comes my man.

Mercutio
   But I'll be hang'd, sir, if he wear your livery:
   Marry, go before to field, he'll be your follower;   55
   Your worship in that sense may call him man.

Tybalt
   Romeo, the love I bear thee can afford
   No better term than this—thou art a villain.

Romeo
   Tybalt, the reason that I have to love thee
   Doth much excuse the appertaining rage   60
   To such a greeting: villain am I none;
   Therefore farewell; I see thou know'st me not.

Tybalt
   Boy, this shall not excuse the injuries
   That thou hast done me; therefore turn and draw.

Romeo
   I do protest, I never injur'd thee,   65
   But love thee better than thou canst devise

68 **tender**   cherish.

71 **Alla stoccata**   fencing term; Tybalt is so called by virtue
    of his overt hostility.
    carries it away   wins the day.

72 **ratcatcher**   that is, cat.
    will you walk?   invitation to duel.

75 **make bold withal**   assault.

76 **dry-beat**   thrash.

77 **pilcher**   scabbard.

78 **ears**   hilts.

88 **sped**   destroyed.

Till thou shalt know the reason of my love:
And so, good Capulet—which name I tender
As dearly as mine own—be satisfied.

Mercutio
O calm, dishonorable, vile submission!   70
Alla stoccata carries it away.

> [*Draws.*

Tybalt, you ratcatcher, will you walk?

Tybalt
What wouldst thou have with me?

Mercutio
Good king of cats, nothing but one of your nine lives,
that I mean to make bold withal, and, as you shall use   75
me hereafter, dry-beat the rest of the eight. Will you
pluck your sword out of his pilcher by the ears? make
haste, lest mine be about your ears ere it be out.

Tybalt
I am for you.

> [*Drawing.*

Romeo
Gentle Mercutio, put thy rapier up.   80

Mercutio
Come, sir, your passado.

> [*They fight.*

Romeo
Draw, Benvolio; beat down their weapons.
Gentlemen, for shame, forbear this outrage!
Tybalt, Mercutio, the prince expressly hath
Forbid this bandying in Verona streets: 85
Hold Tybalt! good Mercutio!

> [*Tybalt under Romeo's arms stabs Mercutio and*
> *flies with his followers.*

Mercutio
                    I am hurt;
A plague o' both your houses! I am sped:

96 **peppered**   finished.

100 **the book of arithmetic**   that is, the rules of fencing theory.

107 **ally**   relative.
108 **very**   true.

113 **temper**   state of mind.

Is he gone, and hath nothing?

Benvolio

What, art thou hurt?   90

Mercutio

Aye, aye, a scratch, a scratch; marry, 'tis enough.
Where is my page? Go, villain, fetch a surgeon.

[*Exit Page.*

Romeo

Courage, man; the hurt cannot be much.

Mercutio

No, 'tis not so deep as a well, nor so wide as a church
door; but 'tis enough, 'twill serve: ask for me tomor-   95
row, and you shall find me a grave man. I am peppered,
I warrant, for this world. A plague o' both your houses!
'Zounds, a dog, a rat, a mouse, a cat, to scratch a man
to death! a braggart, a rogue, a villain, that fights by
the book of arithmetic! Why the devil came you be-   100
tween us? I was hurt under your arm.

Romeo

I thought all for the best.

Mercutio

Help me into some house, Benvolio,
Or I shall faint. A plague o' both your houses!
They have made worms' meat of me: I have it,   105
And soundly too: your houses!

[*Exeunt Mercutio and Benvolio.*

Romeo

This gentleman, the prince's near ally,
My very friend, hath got this mortal hurt
In my behalf; my reputation stain'd
With Tybalt's slander—Tybalt, that an hour   110
Hath been my kinsman: O sweet Juliet,
Thy beauty hath made me effeminate,
And in my temper soften'd valor's steel!

Reenter Benvolio.

114 **brave** noble.
115 **aspir'd** soared to.

121 **respective** considerate.
    lenity leniency.
122 **conduct** conductor.

132 **up** up in arms.
133 **amaz'd** dumbstruck.
    doom condemn to.

135 **fool** plaything.

Benvolio

    O Romeo, Romeo, brave Mercutio's dead!
    That gallant spirit hath aspir'd the clouds,   115
    Which too untimely here did scorn the earth.

Romeo

    This day's black fate on more days doth depend;
    This but begins the woe others must end.

    Reenter Tybalt.

Benvolio

    Here comes the furious Tybalt back again.

Romeo

    Alive, in triumph! and Mercutio slain!   120
    Away to heaven, respective lenity,
    And fire-ey'd fury be my conduct now!
    Now, Tybalt, take the "villain" back again
    That late thou gavest me; for Mercutio's soul
    Is but a little way above our heads,   125
    Staying for thine to keep him company:
    Either thou, or I, or both, must go with him.

Tybalt

    Thou, wretched boy, that didst consort him here,
    Shalt with him hence.

Romeo

                 This shall determine that.   130
                     [They fight; Tybalt falls.

Benvolio

    Romeo, away, be gone!
    The citizens are up, and Tybalt slain:
    Stand not amaz'd: the prince will doom thee death
    If thou art taken: hence, be gone, away!

Romeo

    O, I am fortune's fool!   135

Benvolio

                 Why dost thou stay?
                       [Exit Romeo.

143 **discover** reveal.
144 **manage** conduct.

154 **fair** civilly.   **bethink** consider.
155 **nice** trifling.
    withal at the same time.

158 **take truce with** come to terms with.
159 **tilts** thrusts.

Enter Citizens.

First Citizen
Which way ran he that kill'd Mercutio?
Tybalt, that murderer, which way ran he?
Benvolio
There lies that Tybalt.
First Citizen
                              Up, sir, go with me;   140
I charge thee in the prince's name, obey.

*Enter Prince, attended; Montague, Capulet, their
Wives, and others.*

Prince
Where are the vile beginners of this fray?
Benvolio
O noble prince, I can discover all.
The unlucky manage of this fatal brawl:
There lies the man, slain by young Romeo,   145
That slew thy kinsman, brave Mercutio.
Lady Capulet
Tybalt, my cousin! O my brother's child!
O prince! O cousin! husband! O, the blood is spilt.
Of my dear kinsman! Prince, as thou art true,
For blood of ours, shed blood of Montague.   150
O cousin, cousin!
Prince
Benvolio, who began this bloody fray?
Benvolio
Tybalt, here slain, whom Romeo's hand did slay;
Romeo that spoke him fair, bid him bethink
How nice the quarrel was, and urg'd withal   155
Your high displeasure: all this uttered
With gentle breath, calm look, knees humbly bow'd,
Could not take truce with the unruly spleen
Of Tybalt deaf to peace, but that he tilts

169 **envious**   malicious.
170 **stout**   brave.

With piercing steel at bold Mercutio's breast;   160
Who, all as hot, turns deadly point to point,
And, with a martial scorn, with one hand beats
Cold death aside, and with the other sends
It back to Tybalt, whose dexterity
Retorts it: Romeo he cries aloud,   165
"Hold, friends! friends, part!" and, swifter than his
    tongue,
His agile arm beats down their fatal points,
And 'twixt them rushes; underneath whose arm
An envious thrust from Tybalt hit the life
Of stout Mercutio, and then Tybalt fled: 170
But by and by comes back to Romeo,
Who had but newly entertain'd revenge,
And to't they go like lightning: for, ere I
Could draw to part them, was stout Tybalt slain;
And, as he fell, did Romeo turn and fly;   175
This is the truth, or let Benvolio die.

Lady Capulet
He is a kinsman to the Montague,
Affection makes him false, he speaks not true:
Some twenty of them fought in this black strife,
And all those twenty could but kill one life.   180
I beg for justice, which thou, prince, must give;
Romeo slew Tybalt, Romeo must not live.

Prince
Romeo slew him, he slew Mercutio;
Who now the price of his dear blood doth owe?

Montague
Not Romeo, prince, he was Mercutio's friend;   185
His fault concludes but what the law should end,
The life of Tybalt.

Prince
                    And for that offense
Immediately we do exile him hence:
I have an interest in your hate's proceeding,   190

192 **amerce**   punish.

195 **purchase out**   buy pardon for.

*Soliloquy – talking to yourself
– while alone*

1 **apace**   quickly.
2 **Phoebus**   Phoebus Apollo, the sun god.
3 **Phaethon**   Phoebus' son who was unable to control the
horses of the sun's chariot.

6 **runaway's eyes**   possibly a reference to the sun.
wink   shut.

10 **civil**   courteous.

14 **Hood**   cover.
unmann'd   untrained.
bating   fluttering.

My blood for your rude brawls doth lie a-bleeding;
But I'll amerce you with so strong a fine,
That you shall all repent the loss of mine:
I will be deaf to pleading and excuses;
Nor tears nor prayers shall purchase out abuses: 195
Therefore use none: let Romeo hence in haste,
Else, when he's found, that hour is his last.
Bear hence this body, and attend our will:
Mercy but murders, pardoning those that kill.

                                          [*Exeunt.*

Scene 2. *Capulet's orchard*

Enter Juliet

Juliet

Gallop apace, you fiery-footed steeds,
Towards Phœbus' lodging: such a wagoner
As Phaethon would whip you to the west,
And bring in cloudy night immediately.
Spread thy close curtain, love-performing night,   5
That runaways' eyes may wink, and Romeo
Leap to these arms, untalk'd of and unseen.
Lovers can see to do their amorous rites
By their own beauties; or, if love be blind,
It best agrees with night. Come, civil night,   10
Thou sober-suited matron, all in black,
And learn me how to lose a winning match,
Play'd for a pair of stainless maidenhoods:
Hood my unmann'd blood bating in my cheeks
With thy black mantle, till strange love grown bold   15
Think true love acted simple modesty.
Come, night, come, Romeo, come, thou day in night;

25 **garish**   glaring.

Stage direction   **cords**   rope ladder.

38 **well-a-day!**   alas.

For thou wilt lie upon the wings of night
Whiter than new snow on a raven's back.
Come, gentle night, come, loving, black-brow'd night,   20
Give me my Romeo; and, when he shall die,
Take him and cut him out in little stars,
And he will make the face of heaven so fine,
That all the world will be in love with night,
And pay no worship to the garish sun.   25
O, I have bought the mansion of a love,
But not possess'd it, and, though I am sold,
Not yet enjoy'd; so tedious is this day
As is the night before some festival
To an impatient child that hath new robes   30
And may not wear them. O, here comes my nurse,
And she brings news, and every tongue that speaks
But Romeo's name speaks heavenly eloquence.

    Enter Nurse, with cords.

Now, nurse, what news? What hast thou there? the
    cords
That Romeo bid thee fetch?   35

Nurse

                  Aye, aye, the cords.
                   [*Throws them down.*

Juliet

Aye me! what news? why dost thou wring thy hands?

Nurse

Ah, well-a-day! he's dead, he's dead, he's dead.
We are undone, lady, we are undone.
Alack the day! he's gone, he's kill'd, he's dead.   40

Juliet

Can heaven be so envious?

Nurse

                 Romeo can,
Though heaven cannot. O Romeo, Romeo!
Who ever would have thought it? Romeo!

47 **"I"** yes.

49 **cockatrice** a fabulous serpent said to kill with a single glance of its eyes.

55 **God save the mark!** God forbid.
56 **corse** corpse.

58 **gore** in a clot of.
swounded swooned.

61 **vile earth** wretched body.
resign yield.

Juliet

   What devil art thou that dost torment me thus?   45
   This torture should be roar'd in dismal hell.
   Hath Romeo slain himself? say thou but "I,"
   And that bare vowel "I" shall poison more
   Than the death-darting eye of cockatrice:
   I am not I, if there be such an I,   50
   Or those eyes shut, that make thee answer "I."
   If he be slain, say "I"; or if not, no:
   Brief sounds determine of my weal or woe.

Nurse

   I saw the wound, I saw it with mine eyes—
   God save the mark!—here on his manly breast: 55
   A piteous corse, a bloody piteous corse;
   Pale, pale as ashes, all bedaub'd in blood,
   All in gore blood: I swounded at the sight.

Juliet

   O, break, my heart! poor bankrupt, break at once!
   To prison, eyes, ne'er look on liberty!   60
   Vile earth, to earth resign, end motion here,
   And thou and Romeo press one heavy bier!

Nurse

   O Tybalt, Tybalt, the best friend I had!
   O courteous Tybalt, honest gentleman!
   That ever I should live to see thee dead!   65

Juliet

   What storm is this that blows so contrary?
   Is Romeo slaughter'd, and is Tybalt dead?
   My dear-lov'd cousin, and my dearer lord?
   Then, dreadful trumpet, sound the general doom!
   For who is living, if those two are gone?   70

Nurse

   Tybalt is gone, and Romeo banished;
   Romeo that kill'd him, he is banished.

Juliet

   O God! did Romeo's hand shed Tybalt's blood?

76 **keep** guard.
77 **tyrant** usurper.

79 **substance** reality.
   show appearance.
80 **justly** truly.

83 **bower** lodge.

90 **forsworn** oath-breaking.
   naught wicked.
91 **aqua vitae** spirits, probably brandy.

102 **smooth** speak well of.

Nurse
  It did, it did; alas the day, it did!
Juliet
  O serpent heart, hid with a flow'ring face!   75
  Did ever dragon keep so fair a cave?
  Beautiful tyrant! fiend angelical!
  Dove-feather'd raven, wolvish-ravening lamb!
  Despiscd substance of divinest show!
  Just opposite to what thou justly seem'st,   80
  A damned saint, an honorable villain!
  O nature, what hadst thou to do in hell,
  When thou didst bower the spirit of a fiend
  In mortal paradise of such sweet flesh?
  Was ever book containing such vile matter   85
  So fairly bound? O, that deceit should dwell
  In such a gorgeous palace!
Nurse
                   There's no trust,
  No faith, no honesty in men; all perjur'd,
  All forsworn, all naught, all dissemblers.   90
  Ah, where's my man? give me some aqua vitæ:
  These griefs, these woes, these sorrows make me old.
  Shame come to Romco!
Juliet
                 Blister'd be thy tongue
  For such a wish! he was not born to shame: 95
  Upon his brow shame is asham'd to sit;
  For 'tis a throne where honor may be crown'd
  Sole monarch of the universal earth.
  O, what a beast was I to chide at him!
Nurse
  Will you speak well of him that kill'd your cousin?   100
Juliet
  Shall I speak ill of him that is my husband?
  Ah, poor my lord, what tongue shall smooth thy name,
  When I, thy three-hours wife, have mangled it?

104 **wherefore**   why.

113 **fain**   gladly.

121 **needly**   of necessity.

124 **modern**   ordinary.
125 **rearward**   rear guard.

But wherefore, villain, didst thou kill my cousin?
That villain cousin would have kill'd my husband: 105
Back, foolish tears, back to your native spring;
Your tributary drops belong to woe,
Which you mistaking offer up to joy.
My husband lives, that Tybalt would have slain;
And Tybalt's dead, that would have slain my husband: 110
All this is comfort; wherefore weep I then?
Some word there was, worser than Tybalt's death,
That murder'd me: I would forget it fain;
But, O, it presses to my memory,
Like damned guilty deeds to sinners' minds: 115
"Tybalt is dead, and Romeo banished";
That "banished," that one word "banished,"
Hath slain ten thousand Tybalts. Tybalt's death
Was woe enough, if it had ended there:
Or, if sour woe delights in fellowship,   120
And needly will be rank'd with other griefs,
Why follow'd not, when she said "Tybalt's dead,"
Thy father, or thy mother, nay, or both,
Which modern lamentation might have mov'd?
But with a rearward following Tybalt's death,   125
"Romeo is banished": to speak that word
Is father, mother, Tybalt, Romeo, Juliet,
All slain, all dead. "Romeo is banished."
There is no end, no limit, measure, bound,
In that word's death; no words can that woe sound.   130
Where is my father, and my mother, nurse?

Nurse

Weeping and wailing over Tybalt's corse:
Will you go to them? I will bring you thither.

Juliet

Wash they his wounds with tears: mine shall be spent,
When theirs are dry, for Romeo's banishment.   135
Take up those cords: poor ropes, you are beguil'd,
Both you and I; for Romeo is exil'd:

143 **wot**   know.

2 **parts**   endowments.

9 **doom**   judgment.

He made you for a highway to my bed;
But I, a maid, die maiden-widowed.
Come, cords; come, nurse; I'll to my wedding bed;   140
And death, not Romeo, take my maidenhead!

Nurse

Hie to your chamber: I'll find Romeo
To comfort you: I wot well where he is.
Hark ye, your Romeo will be here at night:
I'll to him; he is hid at Laurence' cell.   145

Juliet

O, find him! give this ring to my true knight,
And bid him come to take his last farewell.

                                                  [*Exeunt.*

Scene 3. Friar Laurence's cell

Enter Friar Laurence.

Friar Laurence

Romeo, come forth; come forth, thou fearful man:
Affliction is enamor'd of thy parts,
And thou are wedded to calamity.

Enter Romeo.

Romeo

Father, what news? what is the prince's doom?
What sorrow craves acquaintance at my hand,   5
That I yet know not?

Friar Laurence
                                Too familiar
Is my dear son with such sour company:
I bring thee tidings of the prince's doom.

Romeo

What less than doomsday is the prince's doom?   10

11 **vanish'd** was issued.

17 **patient** calm.

18 **without** outside.

21 **world's** from the world.

27 **rush'd** thrust.

29 **dear** extraordinary.

34 **validity** value.
35 **courtship** courtliness.

39 **vestal** virginal.

Friar Laurence
  A gentler judgment vanish'd from his lips,
  Not body's death, but body's banishment.

Romeo
  Ha, banishment! be merciful, say "death";
  For exile hath more terror in his look,
  Much more than death: do not say "banishment."   15

Friar Laurence
  Here from Verona art thou banished:
  Be patient, for the world is broad and wide.

Romeo
  There is no world without Verona walls,
  But purgatory, torture, hell itself.
  Hence banished is banish'd from the world,   20
  And world's exile is death: then "banished"
  Is death misterm'd: calling death "banished,"
  Thou cut'st my head off with a golden ax,
  And smilest upon the stroke that murders me.

Friar Laurence
  O deadly sin! O rude unthankfulness!   25
  Thy fault our law calls death; but the kind prince,
  Taking thy part, hath rush'd aside the law,
  And turn'd that black word death to banishment:
  This is dear mercy, and thou seest it not.

Romeo
  'Tis torture, and not mercy: heaven is here,   30
  Where Juliet lives; and every cat and dog
  And little mouse, every unworthy thing,
  Live here in heaven and may look on her,
  But Romeo may not: more validity,
  More honorable state, more courtship lives   35
  In carrion flies than Romeo: they may seize
  On the white wonder of dear Juliet's hand,
  And steal immortal blessing from her lips;
  Who, even in pure and vestal modesty,
  Still blush, as thinking their own kisses sin;   40

46 **mean**   means.
   so mean   base.

53 **fond**   foolish.

But Romeo may not; he is banished:
This may flies do, but I from this must fly:
They are free men, but I am banished:
And say'st thou yet, that exile is not death?
Hadst thou no poison mix'd, no sharp-ground knife,   45
No sudden mean of death, though ne'er so mean,
But "banished" to kill me?—"Banished"?
O friar, the damned use that word in hell;
Howling attends it: how hast thou the heart,
Being a divine, a ghostly confessor,   50
A sin-absolver, and my friend profess'd,
To mangle me with that word "banished"?

Friar Laurence
Thou fond mad man, hear me but speak a word.

Romeo
O, thou wilt speak again of banishment.

Friar Laurence
I'll give thee armor to keep off that word;   55
Adversity's sweet milk, philosophy,
To comfort thee, though thou art banished.

Romeo
Yet "banished"? Hang up philosophy!
Unless philosophy can make a Juliet,
Displant a town, reverse a prince's doom,   60
It helps not, it prevails not: talk no more.

Friar Laurence
O, then I see that madmen have no ears.

Romeo
How should they, when that wise men have no eyes?

Friar Laurence
Let me dispute with thee of thy estate.

Romeo
Thou canst not speak of that thou dost not feel: 65
Wert thou as young as I, Juliet thy love,
An hour but married, Tybalt murdered,
Doting like me, and like me banished,

Then might'st thou speak, then might'st thou tear thy
    hair,
And fall upon the ground, as I do now,   70
Taking the measure of an unmade grave.

                     [*Knocking within.*

Friar Laurence
Arise; one knocks; good Romeo, hide thyself.

Romeo
Not I; unless the breath of heartsick groans
Mist-like infold me from the search of eyes.

                          [*Knocking.*

Friar Laurence
Hark, how they knock! Who's there? Romeo arise;   75
Thou wilt be taken—Stay awhile!—Stand up;

                          [*Knocking.*

Run to my study—By and by!—God's will,
What simpleness is this!—I come, I come!

                          [*Knocking.*

Who knocks so hard? whence come you? what's your
    will?

Nurse
    [*Within*] Let me come in, and you shall know my
        crrand;   80
I come from Lady Juliet.

Friar Laurence
                Welcome, then.

    Enter Nurse.

Nurse
O holy friar, O, tell me, holy friar,
Where is my lady's lord, where's Romeo?

Friar Laurence
There on the ground, with his own tears made drunk.   85

Nurse
O, he is even in my mistress' case,
Just in her case!

88 **woeful sympathy** sorrowful agreement.

94 **O** lament.

98 **old** hardened, experienced.

108 **level** aim.

Friar Laurence
                    O woeful sympathy!
  Piteous predicament!

Nurse
                           Even so lies she,   90
  Blubbering and weeping, weeping and blubbering.
  Stand up, stand up; stand, an you be a man:
  For Juliet's sake, for her sake, rise and stand;
  Why should you fall into so deep an O?

Romeo
  Nurse!   95

Nurse
  Ah sir! ah sir! Well, death's the end of all.

Romeo
  Spakest thou of Juliet? how is it with her?
  Doth she not think me an old murderer,
  Now I have stain'd the childhood of our joy
  With blood remov'd but little from her own?   100
  Where is she? and how doth she? and what says
  My conceal'd lady to our cancel'd love?

Nurse
  O, she says nothing, sir, but weeps and weeps;
  And now falls on her bed; and then starts up,
  And Tybalt calls; and then on Romeo cries,   105
  And then down falls again.

Romeo
                          As if that name,
  Shot from the deadly level of a gun,
  Did murder her, as that name's cursed hand
  Murder'd her kinsman. O, tell me, friar, tell me,   110
  In what vile part of this anatomy
  Doth my name lodge? tell me, that I may sack
  The hateful mansion.
                              [*Drawing his sword.*

Friar Laurence
                          Hold thy desperate hand:
  Art thou a man? thy form cries out thou art: 115

119 **ill-beseeming** unbecoming, inappropriate.

121 **temper'd** mixed, balanced.

125 **rail'st** complain.

143 **There** in that respect.
happy fortunate.

152 **decreed** arranged.

Thy tears are womanish; thy wild acts denote
The unreasonable fury of a beast:
Unseemly woman in a seeming man!
Or ill-beseeming beast in seeming both!
Thou hast amaz'd me: by my holy order,   120
I thought thy disposition better temper'd.
Hast thou slain Tybalt? wilt thou slay thyself?
And slay thy lady that in thy life lives,
By doing damned hate upon thyself?
Why rail'st thou on thy birth, the heaven and earth?   125
Since birth and heaven and earth, all three do meet
In thee at once, which thou at once wouldst lose.
Fie, fie, thou shamest thy shape, thy love, thy wit;
Which, like a usurer, abound'st in all,
And usest none in that true use indeed   130
Which should bedeck thy shape, thy love, thy wit:
Thy noble shape is but a form of wax,
Digressing from the valor of a man;
Thy dear love sworn, but hollow perjury,
Killing that love which thou hast vow'd to cherish;   135
Thy wit, that ornament to shape and love,
Misshapen in the conduct of them both,
Like powder in a skilless soldier's flask,
Is set afire by thine own ignorance,
And thou dismember'd with thine own defense.   140
What, rouse thee, man! thy Juliet is alive,
For whose dear sake thou wast but lately dead;
There art thou happy: Tybalt would kill thee,
But thou slew'st Tybalt; there art thou happy too:
The law, that threaten'd death, becomes thy friend,   145
And turns it to exile; there art thou happy:
A pack of blessings lights upon thy back;
Happiness courts thee in her best array;
But, like a misbehav'd and sullen wench,
Thou pout'st upon thy fortune and thy love: 150
Take heed, take heed, for such die miserable.
Go, get thee to thy love, as was decreed,
Ascend her chamber, hence and comfort her:

154 **watch be set** guards are posted.

157 **blaze** announce.
friends families.

171 **comfort** happiness.

172 **here stands all your state** this is your whole situation.

179 **But** were it not that.
180 **were** would be.

But look thou stay not till the watch be set,
For then thou canst not pass to Mantua;   155
Where thou shalt live till we can find a time
To blaze your marriage, reconcile your friends,
Beg pardon of the prince, and call thee back
With twenty hundred thousand times more joy
Than thou went'st forth in lamentation.   160
Go before, nurse: commend me to thy lady,
And bid her hasten all the house to bed,
Which heavy sorrow makes them apt unto:
Romeo is coming.

Nurse

O Lord, I could have stay'd here all the night   165
To hear good counsel: O, what learning is!
My lord, I'll tell my lady you will come.

Romeo

Do so, and bid my sweet prepare to chide.

Nurse

Here, sir, a ring she bid me give you, sir:
Hie you, make haste, for it grows very late.   170

                [*Exit.*

Romeo

How well my comfort is reviv'd by this!

Friar Laurence

Go hence; good night; and here stands all your state:
Either be gone before the watch be set,
Or by the break of day disguis'd from hence:
Sojourn in Mantua; I'll find out your man,   175
And he shall signify from time to time
Every good hap to you that chances here:
Give me thy hand; 'tis late: farewell; good night.

Romeo

But that a joy past joy calls out on me,
It were a grief, so brief to part with thee: 180
Farewell.

                [*Exeunt.*

1 **fall'n out** happened.
2 **move** urge.

11 **mew'd up** shut up.

12 **desperate** rash.
   tender offer.

16 **son** intended son-in-law.

24 **ado** ceremony.

Scene 4. A room in Capulet's house

Enter Capulet, Lady Capulet, and Paris.

Capulet
  Things have fall'n out, sir, so unluckily,
  That we have had no time to move our daughter.
  Look you, she lov'd her kinsman Tybalt dearly,
  And so did I. Well, we were born to die.
  'Tis very late; she'll not come down tonight: 5
  I promise you, but for your company,
  I would have been abed an hour ago.
Paris
  These times of woe afford no time to woo.
  Madam, good night; commend me to your daughter.
Lady Capulet
  I will, and know her mind early tomorrow;   10
  Tonight she's mew'd up to her heaviness.
Capulet
  Sir Paris, I will make a desperate tender
  Of my child's love: I think she will be rul'd
  In all respects by me; nay more, I doubt it not.
  Wife, go you to her ere you go to bed;   15
  Acquaint her here of my son Paris' love;
  And bid her, mark you me, on Wednesday next—
  But, soft! what day is this?
Paris
                    Monday, my lord.
Capulet
  Monday! ha, ha! Well, Wednesday is too soon;   20
  O' Thursday let it be: o' Thursday, tell her,
  She shall be married to this noble earl.
  Will you be ready? do you like this haste?
  We'll keep no great ado; a friend or two;

26 **carelessly**   in little regard.

33 **against**   for.

35 **Afore me**   my word, a casual oath.

8 **severing**   scattering.
9 **Night's candles**   the stars.

For, hark you, Tybalt being slain so late,   25
It may be thought we held him carelessly,
Being our kinsman, if we revel much:
Therefore we'll have some half a dozen friends,
And there an end. But what say you to Thursday?

Paris

My lord, I would that Thursday were tomorrow.   30

Capulet

Well, get you gone: o' Thursday be it then.
Go you to Juliet ere you go to bed,
Prepare her, wife, against this wedding day.
Farewell, my lord. Light to my chamber, ho!
Afore me, it is so very very late,   35
That we may call it early by and by:
Good night.

                                                    [*Exeunt.*

Scene 5. *Capulet's orchard*

Enter Romeo and Juliet, above, at the window.

Juliet

Wilt thou be gone? it is not yet near day:
It was the nightingale, and not the lark,
That pierc'd the fearful hollow of thine ear;
Nightly she sings on yond pomegranate tree:
Believe me, love, it was the nightingale.   5

Romeo

It was the lark, the herald of the morn,
No nightingale: look, love, what envious streaks
Do lace the severing clouds in yonder east:
Night's candles are burnt out, and jocund day
Stands tiptoe on the misty mountain tops: 10
I must be gone and live, or stay and die.

18 **so** if.

20 **reflex** reflection.
   Cynthia the moon.
22 **vaulty** vaulted.
23 **care** desire.

28 **sharps** shrill high notes.
29 **division** melody.

31 **Some say ... change eyes** because the ugly toad has
   beautiful eyes while the beautiful lark has ugly ones.
33 **affray** frighten.
34 **hunt's-up** an early morning song to arouse hunters.

Juliet
    Yond light is not daylight, I know it, I:
    It is some meteor that the sun exhales,
    To be to thee this night a torchbearer,
    And light thee on thy way to Mantua: 15
    Therefore stay yet; thou need'st not to be gone.

Romeo
    Let me be ta'en, let me be put to death;
    I am content, so thou wilt have it so.
    I'll say yon gray is not the morning's eye,
    'Tis but the pale reflex of Cynthia's brow;   20
    Nor that is not the lark, whose notes do beat
    The vaulty heaven so high above our heads:
    I have more care to stay than will to go:
    Come, death, and welcome! Juliet wills it so.
    How is't my soul? let's talk: it is not day.   25

Juliet
    It is, it is: hie hence, be gone, away!
    It is the lark that sings so out of tune,
    Straining harsh discords and unpleasing sharps.
    Some say the lark makes sweet division;
    This doth not so, for she divideth us: 30
    Some say the lark and loathed toad change eyes;
    O, now I would they had chang'd voices too!
    Since arm from arm that voice doth us affray,
    Hunting thee hence with hunt's-up to the day.
    O, now be gone; more light and light it grows.   35

Romeo
    More light and light: more dark and dark our woes!

    Enter Nurse, to the chamber.

Nurse
    Madam!

Juliet
    Nurse?

46 **count**   method of reckoning.
   much in years   greatly aged.

54 **ill-divining**   foreseeing evil.

59 **Dry sorrow drinks our blood**   grief was thought to exhaust
   the blood.

Nurse
Your lady mother is coming to your chamber:
The day is broke; be wary, look about.   40

                         [*Exit*.

Juliet
Then, window, let day in, and let life out.

Romeo
Farewell, farewell! one kiss, and I'll descend.

                     [*Descends*.

Juliet
Art thou gone so? my lord, my love, my friend!
I must hear from thee every day in the hour,
For in a minute there are many days: 45
O, by this count I shall be much in years
Ere I again behold my Romeo!

Romeo
Farewell!
I will omit no opportunity
That may convey my greetings, love, to thee.   50

Juliet
O, think'st thou we shall ever meet again?

Romeo
I doubt it not; and all these woes shall serve
For sweet discourses in our time to come.

Juliet
O God! I have an ill-divining soul.
Methinks I see thee, now thou art below,   55
As one dead in the bottom of a tomb:
Either my eyesight fails or thou look'st pale.

Romeo
And trust me, love, in my eye so do you:
Dry sorrow drinks our blood. Adieu, adieu!

                         [*Exit*.

Juliet
O fortune, fortune! all men call thee fickle: 60

76 feeling heartfelt.

If thou art fickle, what dost thou with him
That is renown'd for faith? Be fickle, fortune;
For then, I hope, thou wilt not keep him long,
But send him back.

Lady Capulet
[*Within*]   Ho, daughter! are you up?   65

Juliet
Who is't that calls? it is my lady mother!
Is she not down so late, or up so early?
What unaccustom'd cause procures her hither?

    Enter Lady Capulet.

Lady Capulet
Why, how now, Juliet!

Juliet
                Madam, I am not well.   70

Lady Capulet
Evermore weeping for your cousin's death?
What, wilt thou wash him from his grave with tears?
An if thou couldst, thou couldst not make him live;
Therefore have done: some grief shows much of love,
But much of grief shows still some want of wit.   75

Juliet
Yet let me weep for such a feeling loss.

Lady Capulet
So shall you feel the loss, but not the friend
Which you weep for.

Juliet
              Feeling so the loss,
I cannot choose but ever weep the friend.   80

Lady Capulet
Well, girl, thou weep'st not so much for his death
As that the villain lives which slaughter'd him.

Juliet
What villain, madam?

93 **runagate**   renegade.

101 **temper**   mix.

105 **wreak**   avenge.

Lady Capulet
>   That same villain, Romeo.

Juliet
[*Aside*]   Villain and he be many miles asunder.   85
God pardon him! I do, with all my heart;
And yet no man like he doth grieve my heart.

Lady Capulet
That is because the traitor murderer lives.

Juliet
Aye, madam, from the reach of these my hands:
Would none but I might venge my cousin's death!   90

Lady Capulet
We will have vengeance for it, fear thou not:
Then weep no more. I'll send to one in Mantua,
Where that same banish'd runagate doth live,
Shall give him such an unaccustom'd dram
That he shall soon keep Tybalt company: 95
And then, I hope, thou wilt be satisfied.

Juliet
Indeed, I never shall be satisfied
With Romeo, till I behold him—dead—
Is my poor heart so for a kinsman vex'd.
Madam, if you could find out but a man   100
To bear a poison, I would temper it,
That Romeo should, upon receipt thereof,
Soon sleep in quiet. O, how my heart abhors
To hear him nam'd, and cannot come to him,
To wreak the love I bore my cousin   105
Upon his body that hath slaughter'd him!

Lady Capulet
Find thou the means, and I'll find such a man.
But now I'll tell thee joyful tidings, girl.

Juliet
And joy comes well in such a needy time:
What are they, I beseech your ladyship?   110

111 **careful** concerned.

113 **sorted out** selected.

115 **in happy time** how opportune.

133 **conduit** fountain.

Lady Capulet

   Well, well, thou hast a careful father, child;
   One who, to put thee from thy heaviness,
   Hath sorted out a sudden day of joy,
   That thou expect'st not, nor I look'd not for.

Juliet

   Madam, in happy time, what day is that?   115

Lady Capulet

   Marry, my child, early next Thursday morn,
   The gallant, young, and noble gentleman,
   The County Paris, at Saint Peter's Church,
   Shall happily make thee there a joyful bride.

Juliet

   Now, by Saint Peter's Church, and Peter too,   120
   He shall not make me there a joyful bride.
   I wonder at this haste; that I must wed
   Ere he that should be husband comes to woo.
   I pray you, tell my lord and father, madam,
   I will not marry yet; and, when I do, I swear,   125
   It shall be Romeo, whom you know I hate,
   Rather than Paris. These are news indeed!

Lady Capulet

   Here comes your father; tell him so yourself,
   And see how he will take it at your hands.

    Enter Capulet and Nurse.

Capulet

   When the sun sets, the air doth drizzle dew;   130
   But for the sunset of my brother's son
   It rains downright.
   How now! a conduit, girl? what, still in tears?
   Evermore showering? In one little body
   Thou counterfeit'st a bark, a sea, a wind: 135
   For still thy eyes, which I may call the sea,
   Do ebb and flow with tears; the bark thy body is,
   Sailing in this salt flood; the winds, thy sighs;
   Who raging with thy tears, and they with them,

143 **she will none**   she will have none of it.

145 **take me with you**   let me understand you.

148 **wrought**   arranged for.

153 **chop-logic**   quibbler.

155 **minion**   spoiled darling.

157 **fettle**   prepare.

159 **hurdle**   wooden frame or sledge on which criminals were transported to their place of execution.
160 **green-sickness**   anemia affecting adolescents.
carrion   lump of flesh.

164 **but to**   just long enough to.

Without a sudden calm will overset   140
Thy tempest-tossed body. How now, wife!
Have you deliver'd to her our decree?

Lady Capulet

Aye, sir; but she will none, she gives you thanks.
I would the fool were married to her grave!

Capulet

Soft! take me with you, take me with you, wife.   145
How! will she none? doth she not give us thanks?
Is she not proud? doth she not count her blest,
Unworthy as she is, that we have wrought
So worthy a gentleman to be her bridegroom?

Juliet

Not proud, you have, but thankful that you have: 150
Proud can I never be of what I hate;
But thankful even for hate that is meant love.

Capulet

How, how! how, how! chop-logic! What is this?
"Proud," and "I thank you," and "I thank you not";
And yet "not proud": mistress minion, you,   155
Thank me no thankings, nor proud me no prouds,
But fettle your fine joints 'gainst Thursday next,
To go with Paris to Saint Peter's Church,
Or I will drag thee on a hurdle thither.
Out, you green-sickness carrion! out, you baggage!   160
You tallow-face!

Lady Capulet

                Fie, fie! what, are you mad?

Juliet

Good father, I beseech you on my knees,
Hear me with patience but to speak a word.

Capulet

Hang thee, young baggage! disobedient wretch!   165
I tell thee what: get thee to church o' Thursday,
Or never after look me in the face:
Speak not, reply not, do not answer me;

169 **itch**   that is, to hit you.

173 **hilding**   wretch.

175 **rate**   berate.

177 **smatter**   chatter about matters you know nothing about.

182 **gossip's bowl**   a hot punch.

185 **God's bread!**   an oath; the host.

191 **parts**   characteristics.

193 **puling**   whining.
194 **mammet**   doll, puppet.
    in her fortune's tender   on the offer of good fortune.

My fingers itch. Wife, we scarce thought us blest
That God had lent us but this only child;   170
But now I see this one is one too much,
And that we have a curse in having her:
Out on her, hilding!

Nurse

           God in heaven bless her!
You are to blame, my lord, to rate her so.   175

Capulet

And why, my lady wisdom? hold your tongue,
Good prudence; smatter with your gossips, go.

Nurse

I speak no treason.

Capulet

        O, God ye god-den.

Nurse

May not one speak?   180

Capulet

          Peace, you mumbling fool!
Utter your gravity o'er a gossip's bowl;
For here we need it not.

Lady Capulet

          You are too hot

Capulet

God's bread! it makes me mad: 185
Day, night, hour, tide, time, work, play,
Alone, in company, still my care hath been
To have her match'd: and having now provided
A gentleman of noble parentage,
Of fair demesnes, youthful, and nobly train'd,   190
Stuff'd, as they say, with honorable parts,
Proportion'd as one's thought would wish a man;
And then to have a wretched puling fool,
A whining mammet, in her fortune's tender,
To answer "I'll not wed; I cannot love,   195
I am too young; I pray you, pardon me."

197 **pardon you**   give leave to depart.

199 **I do not use**   I am not accustomed.
200 **advise**   consider.

205 **Trust to't**   be assured of it.
    be forsworn   break my oath.

211 **monument**   burial vault.

219 **stratagems**   dreadful deeds.

224 **all the world to nothing**   the odds are all to nothing.
225 **challenge**   claim.

But, an you will not wed, I'll pardon you:
Graze where you will, you shall not house with me:
Look to't, think on't, I do not use to jest.
Thursday is near; lay hand on heart, advise: 200
An you be mine, I'll give you to my friend;
An you be not, hang, beg, starve, die in the streets,
For, by my soul, I'll ne'er acknowledge thee,
Nor what is mine shall never do thee good:
Trust to't, bethink you; I'll not be forsworn.   205

                                                  [*Exit.*

Juliet

Is there no pity sitting in the clouds,
That sees into the bottom of my grief?
O, sweet my mother, cast me not away!
Delay this marriage for a month, a week;
Or, if you do not, make the bridal bed   210
In that dim monument where Tybalt lies.

Lady Capulet

Talk not to me, for I'll not speak a word:
Do as thou wilt, for I have done with thee.

                                                  [*Exit.*

Juliet

O God!—O nurse, how shall this be prevented?
My husband is on earth, my faith in heaven;   215
How shall that faith return again to earth,
Unless that husband send it me from heaven
By leaving earth? comfort me, counsel me.
Alack, alack, that heaven should practice stratagems
Upon so soft a subject as myself!   220
What say'st thou? hast thou not a word of joy?
Some comfort, nurse.

Nurse

                        Faith, here it is.
Romeo is banish'd and all the world to nothing,
That he dares ne'er come back to challenge you;   225
Or, if he do, it needs must be by stealth.
Then, since the case so stands as now it doth,

230 **dishclout**   dishcloth.

232 **Beshrew**   curse.

247 **ancient damnation!**   damned old woman.

252 **bosom**   confidence.

I think it best you married with the county.
O, he's a lovely gentleman!
Romeo's a dishclout to him: an eagle, madam,   230
Hath not so green, so quick, so fair an eye
As Paris hath. Beshrew my very heart,
I think you are happy in this second match,
For it excels your first: or if it did not,
Your first is dead, or 'twere as good he were   235
As living here and you no use of him.

Juliet
Speakest thou from thy heart?

Nurse
                              And from my soul too;
Else beshrew them both.

Juliet
                    Amen!   240

Nurse
                         What?

Juliet
Well, thou hast comforted me marvelous much.
Go in, and tell my lady I am gone,
Having displeas'd my father, to Laurence' cell,
To make confession and to be absolv'd.   245

Nurse
Marry, I will, and this is wisely done.

                                                 [*Exit.*

Juliet
Ancient damnation! O most wicked fiend!
Is it more sin to wish me thus forsworn,
Or to dispraise my lord with that same tongue
Which she hath prais'd him with above compare   250
So many thousand times? Go, counselor;
Thou and my bosom henceforth shall be twain.
I'll to the friar, to know his remedy:
If all else fail, myself have power to die.

                                                 [*Exit.*

2 **father**   intended father-in-law.
3 **nothing slow**   extremely reluctant.

5 **Uneven**   difficult.

10 **sway**   power.

ACT IV

Scene 1. Friar Laurence's cell

Enter Friar Laurence and Paris.

Friar Laurence
On Thursday, sir? the time is very short.
Paris
My father Capulet will have it so;
And I am nothing slow to slack his haste.
Friar Laurence
You say you do not know the lady's mind:
Uneven is the course; I like it not.   5
Paris
Immoderately she weeps for Tybalt's death,
And therefore have I little talk'd of love,
For Venus smiles not in a house of tears.
Now, sir, her father counts it dangerous
That she doth give her sorrow so much sway,   10
And in his wisdom hastes our marriage,
To stop the inundation of her tears,
Which, too much minded by herself alone,
May be put from her by society:
Now do you know the reason of this haste.   15
Friar Laurence
[*Aside*]   I would I knew not why it should be slow'd.—
Look, sir, here comes the lady toward my cell.

    Enter Juliet.

Paris
Happily met, my lady and my wife!

28 **price** value.

30 **abused** disfigured.

32 **spite** injury.

Juliet
>   That may be, sir, when I may be a wife.

Paris
>   That may be must be, love, on Thursday next.   20

Juliet
>   What must be shall be.

Friar Laurence
>   That's a certain text.

Paris
>   Come you to make confession to this father?

Juliet
>   To answer that, I should confess to you.

Paris
>   Do not deny to him that you love me.   25

Juliet
>   I will confess to you that I love him.

Paris
>   So will ye, I am sure, that you love me.

Juliet
>   If I do so, it will be of more price,
>   Being spoke behind your back, than to your face.

Paris
>   Poor soul, thy face is much abused with tears.   30

Juliet
>   The tears have got small victory by that;
>   For it was bad enough before their spite.

Paris
>   Thou wrong'st it more than tears with that report.

Juliet
>   That is no slander, sir, which is a truth,
>   And what I spake, I spake it to my face.   35

Paris
>   Thy face is mine, and thou hast slander'd it.

40 **pensive**   sorrowful.
41 **entreat**   ask to have.

42 **shield**   prevent.

48 **compass**   limit.
49 **prorogue**   postpone.

58 **label**   that is, wax seal.

62 **present**   immediate.

65 **commission**   authority.

Juliet

   It may be so, for it is not mine own.
   Are you at leisure, holy father, now,
   Or shall I come to you at evening mass?

Friar Laurence

   My leisure serves me, pensive daughter, now.   40
   My lord, we must entreat the time alone.

Paris

   God shield I should disturb devotion!
   Juliet, on Thursday early will I rouse ye:
   Till then, adieu, and keep this holy kiss.

                          [*Exit.*

Juliet

   O, shut the door, and when thou hast done so,   45
   Come weep with me; past hope, past cure, past help!

Friar Laurence

   Ah, Juliet, I already know thy grief;
   It strains me past the compass of my wits:
   I hear thou must, and nothing may prorogue it,
   On Thursday next be married to this county.   50

Juliet

   Tell me not, friar, that you hear'st of this,
   Unless thou tell me how I may prevent it:
   If in thy wisdom thou canst give no help,
   Do thou but call my resolution wise,
   And with this knife I'll help it presently.   55
   God join'd my heart and Romeo's, thou our hands;
   And ere this hand, by thee to Romeo's seal'd,
   Shall be the label to another deed,
   Or my true heart with treacherous revolt
   Turn to another, this shall slay them both: 60
   Therefore, out of thy long-experienc'd time,
   Give me some present counsel; or, behold,
   'Twixt my extremes and me this bloody knife
   Shall play the umpire, arbitrating that
   Which the commission of thy years and art   65

75 **chide**   drive.
76 **cop'st**   tries to bargain.

80 **thievish ways**   roads where thieves lurk.

82 **charnel house**   storehouse for bones uncovered when digging new graves.
84 **reeky**   reeking.
chapless   jawless.

96 **presently**   at once.
97 **humor**   fluid.

Could to no issue of true honor bring.
Be not so long to speak; I long to die,
If what thou speak'st speak not of remedy.

Friar Laurence

Hold, daughter: I do spy a kind of hope,
Which craves as desperate an execution   70
As that is desperate which we would prevent.
If, rather than to marry County Paris,
Thou hast the strength of will to slay thyself,
Then is it likely thou wilt undertake
A thing like death to chide away this shame,   75
That cop'st with death himself to 'scape from it;
And, if thou dar'st, I'll give thee remedy.

Juliet

O, bid me leap, rather than marry Paris,
From off the battlements of yonder tower;
Or walk in thievish ways; or bid me lurk   80
Where serpents are; chain me with roaring bears;
Or shut me nightly in a charnel house,
O'ercover'd quite with dead men's rattling bones,
With reeky shanks and yellow chapless skulls;
Or bid me go into a new-made grave,   85
And hide me with a dead man in his shroud;
Things that to hear them told, have made me tremble;
And I will do it without fear or doubt,
To live an unstain'd wife to my sweet love.

Friar Laurence

Hold, then; go home, be merry, give consent   90
To marry Paris: Wednesday is tomorrow;
Tomorrow night look that thou lie alone,
Let not thy nurse lie with thee in thy chamber:
Take thou this vial, being then in bed,
And this distilled liquor drink thou off: 95
When presently through all thy veins shall run
A cold and drowsy humor; for no pulse
Shall keep his native progress, but surcease:

103 **supple government**   facility of movement.

111 **uncover'd**   that is, with uncovered face.

115 **drift**   intention.

120 **inconstant toy**   whim of irresolution.

No warmth, no breath, shall testify thou livest;
The roses in thy lips and cheeks shall fade   100
To paly ashes; thy eyes' windows fall,
Like death, when he shuts up the day of life;
Each part, depriv'd of supple government,
Shall, stiff and stark and cold, appear like death:
And in this borrow'd likeness of shrunk death   105
Thou shalt continue two and forty hours,
And then awake as from a pleasant sleep.
Now, when the bridegroom in the morning comes
To rouse thee from thy bed, there art thou dead:
Then, as the manner of our country is,   110
In thy best robes uncover'd on the bier
Thou shalt be borne to that same ancient vault
Where all the kindred of the Capulets lie.
In the mean time, against thou shalt awake,
Shall Romeo by my letters know our drift;   115
And hither shall he come: and he and I
Will watch thy waking, and that very night
Shall Romeo bear thee hence to Mantua.
And this shall free thee from this present shame,
If no inconstant toy nor womanish fear   120
Abate thy valor in the acting it.

Juliet
Give me, give me! O, tell not me of fear!

Friar Laurence
Hold; get you gone, be strong and prosperous
In this resolve; I'll send a friar with speed
To Mantua, with my letters to thy lord.   125

Juliet
Love give me strength! and strength shall help afford.
Farewell, dear father!
                                          [*Exeunt.*

2 **cunning** skillful.

10 **unfurnish'd** unprovisioned.

14 **peevish** silly.
    harlotry good-for-nothing girl.
    it she.

Scene 2. Hall in Capulet's house

Enter Capulet, Lady Capulet, Nurse, and two Servingmen.

Capulet
So many guests invite as here are writ.
                              [*Exit First Servant.*
Sirrah, go hire me twenty cunning cooks.

Second Servant
You shall have none ill, sir, for I'll try if they can lick
their fingers.

Capulet
How canst thou try them so?   5

Second Servant
Marry, sir, 'tis an ill cook that cannot lick his own
fingers: therefore he that cannot lick his fingers goes
not with me.

Capulet
Go, be gone.
                              [*Exit Second Servant.*
We shall be much unfurnish'd for this time.   10
What, is my daughter gone to Friar Laurence?

Nurse
Aye, forsooth.

Capulet
Well, he may chance to do some good on her:
A peevish self-will'd harlotry it is.

        Enter Juliet.

Nurse
See where she comes from shrift with merry look.   15

24 **knot**   bond of wedlock.

26 **becomed**   befitting.

28 **on't**   of it.

32 **bound**   indebted.

33 **closet**   private chamber.
34 **sort**   select.

Capulet

    How now, my headstrong! where have you been
       gadding?

Juliet

    Where I have learn'd me to repent the sin
    Of disobedient opposition
    To you and your behests, and am enjoin'd
    By holy Laurence to fall prostrate here,   20
    To beg your pardon. Pardon, I beseech you!
    Henceforward I am ever rul'd by you.

Capulet

    Send for the county; go tell him of this:
    I'll have this knot knit up tomorrow morning.

Juliet

    I met the youthful lord at Laurence' cell,   25
    And gave him what becomed love I might,
    Not stepping o'er the bounds of modesty.

Capulet

    Why, I am glad on't; this is well: stand up:
    This is as't should be. Let me see the county;
    Aye, marry, go, I say, and fetch him hither.   30
    Now, afore God, this reverend holy friar,
    All our whole city is much bound to him.

Juliet

    Nurse, will you go with me into my closet,
    To help me sort such needful ornaments
    As you think fit to furnish me tomorrow?   35

Lady Capulet

    No, not till Thursday; there is time enough.

Capulet

    Go, nurse, go with her: we'll to church tomorrow.
                        [*Exeunt Juliet and Nurse.*

Lady Capulet

    We shall be short in our provision:
    'Tis now near night.

46 **up** completely.

3 **orisons** prayers.

5 **cross** contrary.

7 **cull'd** chosen.
8 **behoveful** needful.
  state pomp.

Capulet

                 Tush, I will stir about,   40
And all things shall be well, I warrant thee, wife:
Go thou to Juliet, help to deck up her;
I'll not to bed tonight; let me alone;
I'll play the housewife for this once. What, ho!
They are all forth: well, I will walk myself   45
To County Paris, to prepare him up
Against tomorrow: my heart is wondrous light,
Since this same wayward girl is so reclaim'd.

                                   [*Exeunt.*

Scene 3. *Juliet's chamber*

Enter Juliet and Nurse.

Juliet

    Aye, those attires are best: but, gentle nurse,
I pray thee, leave me to myself tonight;
For I have need of many orisons
To move the heavens to smile upon my state,
Which, well thou know'st, is cross and full of sin.   5

Enter Lady Capulet.

Lady Capulet

    What, are you busy, ho? need you my help?

Juliet

    No, madam; we have cull'd such necessaries
As are behoveful for our state tomorrow:
So please you, let me now be left alone,
And let the nurse this night sit up with you,   10
For I am sure you have your hands full all
In this so sudden business.

Lady Capulet

                  Good night!

16 **faint**   that is, producing faintness in her.

30 **tried**   proven.

38 **conceit**   idea.

43 **green**   recently.

Get thee to bed and rest, for thou hast need.
>   [*Exeunt Lady Capulet and Nurse.*

Juliet

Farewell! God knows when we shall meet again.   15
I have a faint cold fear thrills through my veins,
That almost freezes up the heat of life:
I'll call them back again to comfort me.
Nurse! —What should she do here?
My dismal scene I needs must act alone.   20
Come, vial.
What if this mixture do not work at all?
Shall I be married then tomorrow morning?
No, no: this shall forbid it. Lie thou there.
>   [*Laying down a dagger.*

What if it be a poison, which the friar   25
Subtly hath minister'd to have me dead,
Lest in this marriage he should be dishonor'd,
Because he married me before to Romeo?
I fear it is: and yet, methinks, it should not,
For he hath still been tried a holy man.   30
How if, when I am laid into the tomb,
I wake before the time that Romeo
Come to redeem me? there's a fearful point.
Shall I not then be stifled in the vault,
To whose foul mouth no healthsome air breathes in,   35
And there die strangled ere my Romeo comes?
Or, if I live, is it not very like,
The horrible conceit of death and night,
Together with the terror of the place,
As in a vault, an ancient receptacle,   40
Where for this many hundred years the bones
Of all my buried ancestors are pack'd;
Where bloody Tybalt, yet but green in earth,
Lies festering in his shroud; where, as they say,
At some hours in the night spirits resort;   45
Alack, alack, is it not like that I
So early waking, what with loathsome smells

48 **mandrakes** plants with opiate qualities whose forked roots resemble human legs; when the plant is pulled from the earth, it is supposed to shriek and cause madness in the hearer.

54 **rage** madness.

58 **stay** hold, stay.

2 **pastry** pantry.

5 **Angelica** the nurse.

7 **cot-quean** man meddling with women's work; used contemptuously here.

9 **watching** wakefulness.

And shrieks like mandrakes torn out of the earth.
That living mortals hearing them run mad:
O, if I wake, shall I not be distraught, 50
Environed with all these hideous fears,
And madly play with my forefathers' joints,
And pluck the mangled Tybalt from his shroud,
And, in this rage, with some great kinsman's bone,
As with a club, dash out my desperate brains? 55
O, look! methinks I see my cousin's ghost
Seeking out Romeo, that did spit his body
Upon a rapier's point: stay, Tybalt, stay!
Romeo, I come! this do I drink to thee.
      [She falls upon her bed, within the curtains.

Scene 4. Hall in Capulet's house

Enter Lady Capulet and Nurse.

Lady Capulet
  Hold, take these keys, and fetch more spices, nurse.
Nurse
  They call for dates and quinces in the pastry.

    Enter Capulet.

Capulet
  Come, stir, stir, stir! the second cock hath crow'd,
  The curfew bell hath rung, 'tis three o'clock:
  Look to the baked meats, good Angelica: 5
  Spare not for cost.
Nurse
           Go, you cot-quean, go,
  Get you to bed; faith, you'll be sick tomorrow
  For this night's watching.
Capulet
  No, not a whit: what! I have watch'd ere now 10

12 **mouse-hunt** woman-chaser.

14 **hood** ninny.

22 **Mass** by the Mass.
   whoreson rascal.
23 **loggerhead** blockhead.

All night for lesser cause, and ne'er been sick.

Lady Capulet

    Aye, you have been a mouse-hunt in your time;

    But I will watch you from such watching now.

                [*Exeunt Lady Capulet and Nurse.*

Capulet

    A jealous hood, a jealous hood!

    Enter three or four Servingmen, with spits, and logs,
    and baskets.

                      Now, fellow,   15

    What's there?

First Servant

    Things for the cook, sir, but I know not what.

Capulet

    Make haste, make haste.   [*Exit First Servant*]   Sirrah,
        fetch drier logs:

    Call Peter, he will show thee where they are.

Second Servant

    I have a head, sir, that will find out logs,   20

    And never trouble Peter for the matter.

Capulet

    Mass, and well said; a merry whoreson, ha!

    Thou shalt be loggerhead.   [*Exit Second Servant*]
        Good faith, 'tis day:

    The county will be here with music straight,

    For so he said he would.   [*Music within.*]   I hear
        him near.   25

    Nurse! Wife! What, ho! What, nurse, I say!

    Reenter Nurse.

    Go waken Juliet, go and trim her up;

    I'll go and chat with Paris: hie, make haste,

    Make haste: the bridegroom he is come already:

    Make haste, I say.   30

                        [*Exeunt.*

1 **fast**   fast asleep.

4 **pennyworths**   that is, of sleep.

6 **set up his rest**   firmly resolved.

Scene 5. *Juliet's chamber*

Enter Nurse.

Nurse
Mistress! what, mistress! Juliet! fast, I warrant her, she:
Why, lamb! why, lady! fie, you slug-a-bed!
Why, love, I say! madam! sweetheart! why, bride!
What, not a word? you take your pennyworths now;
Sleep for a week; for the next night, I warrant,   5
The County Paris hath set up his rest
That you shall rest but little. God forgive me,
Marry, and amen, how sound is she asleep!
I needs must wake her. Madam, madam, madam!
Aye, let the county take you in your bed;   10
He'll fright you up, i' faith. Will it not be?
                                        [*Undraws the curtains.*
What, dress'd! and in your clothes! and down again!
I must needs wake you. Lady! lady! lady!
Alas, alas! Help, help! my lady's dead!
O, well-a-day, that ever I was born!   15
Some aqua vitæ, ho! My lord, my lady!

Enter Lady Capulet.

Lady Capulet
What noise is here?
Nurse
                    O lamentable day!
Lady Capulet
What is the matter?
Nurse
                    Look, look! O heavy day!   20
Lady Capulet
O me, O me! My child, my only life,

27 **Out, alas!**   exclamation of sorrow.
28 **settled**   congealed.

43 **living**   material property.

Revive, look up, or I will die with thee.
Help, help! call help.

Enter Capulet.

Capulet
For shame, bring Juliet forth; her lord is come.
Nurse
She's dead, deceas'd, she's dead; alack the day!   25
Lady Capulet
Alack the day, she's dead, she's dead, she's dead!
Capulet
Ha! let me see her. Out, alas! she's cold;
Her blood is settled and her joints are stiff;
Life and these lips have long been separated.
Death lies on her like an untimely frost   30
Upon the sweetest flower of all the field.
Nurse
O lamentable day!
Lady Capulet
                    O woeful time!
Capulet
Death, that hath ta'en her hence to make me wail,
Ties up my tongue and will not let me speak.   35

Enter Friar Laurence and Paris, with Musicians.

Friar Laurence
Come, is the bride ready to go to church?
Capulet
Ready to go, but never to return.
O son, the night before thy wedding day
Hath death lain with thy wife: see, there she lies,
Flower as she was, deflowered by him.   40
Death is my son-in-law, Death is my heir;
My daughter he hath wedded: I will die,
And leave him all; life, living, all is Death's.

44 **thought**   hoped.

51 **catch'd**   snatched.

63 **Uncomfortable**   discomforting.
64 **solemnity**   festivity.

68 **confusion**   disaster.

Paris

    Have I thought long to see this morning's face
    And doth it give me such a sight as this? 45

Lady Capulet

    Accurst, unhappy, wretched, hateful day!
    Most miserable hour that e'er time saw
    In lasting labor of his pilgrimage!
    But one, poor one, one poor and loving child,
    But one thing to rejoice and solace in, 50
    And cruel death hath catch'd it from my sight!

Nurse

    O woe! O woeful, woeful, woeful day!
    Most lamentable day, most woeful day,
    That ever, ever, I did yet behold!
    O day! O day! O day! O hateful day! 55
    Never was seen so black a day as this:
    O woeful day, O woeful day!

Paris

    Beguil'd, divorced, wronged, spited, slain!
    Most detestable death, by thee beguil'd,
    By cruel cruel thee quite overthrown! 60
    O love! O life! not life, but love in death!

Capulet

    Despis'd, distressed, hated, martyr'd, kill'd!
    Uncomfortable time, why camest thou now
    To murder, murder our solemnity?
    O child! O child! my soul, and not my child! 65
    Dead art thou! Alack, my child is dead;
    And with my child my joys are buried!

Friar Laurence

    Peace, ho, for shame! confusion's cure lives not
    In these confusions. Heaven and yourself
    Had part in this fair maid; now heaven hath all, 70
    And all the better is it for the maid:
    Your part in her you could not keep from death;
    But heaven keeps his part in eternal life.

82 **rosemary** a symbol of remembrance used frequently at weddings and funerals.

83 **corse** corpse.

85 **nature** natural feelings.

88 **office** function.

90 **cheer** food.

97 **ill** sin.

99 **put up our pipes** put away our instruments.

101 **case** event.

102 **amended** bettered.

The most you sought was her promotion,
For 'twas your heaven she should be advanc'd: 75
And weep ye now, seeing she is advanc'd
Above the clouds, as high as heaven itself?
O, in this love, you love your child so ill,
That you run mad, seeing that she is well:
She's not well married that lives married long,   80
But she's best married that dies married young.
Dry up your tears, and stick your rosemary
On this fair corse, and, as the custom is,
In all her best array bear her to church:
For though fond nature bids us all lament,   85
Yet nature's tears are reason's merriment.

Capulet

All things that we ordained festival,
Turn from their office to black funeral:
Our instruments to melancholy bells;
Our wedding cheer to a sad burial feast;   90
Our solemn hymns to sullen dirges change;
Our bridal flowers serve for a buried corse,
And all things change them to the contrary.

Friar Laurence

Sir, go you in; and, madam, go with him;
And go, Sir Paris; every one prepare   95
To follow this fair corse unto her grave:
The heavens do low'r upon you for some ill;
Move them no more by crossing their high will.
        [*Exeunt Capulet, Lady Capulet, Paris, and Friar.*

First Musician

Faith, we may put up our pipes, and be gone.

Nurse

Honest good fellows, ah, put up, put up;   100
For, well you know, this is a pitiful case.
                                        [*Exit.*

First Musician

Aye, by my troth, the case may be amended.

103 **"Heart's ease"** a popular song of the day.

107 **dump** mournful song.

112 **give it you** let you have it.
soundly forcefully.

114 **gleek** jeering speech.
114–115 **I will give you the minstrel** I will call you "minstrel,"
an insulting term.

118 **crotchets** whims, also quarter notes in music.

121 **put out** exhibit.

Enter Peter.

Peter
  Musicians, O, musicians, "Heart's ease, Heart's ease":
  O, an you will have me live, play "Heart's ease."

First Musician
  Why "Heart's ease"?   105

Peter
  O, musicians, because my heart itself plays "My heart
  is full of woe": O, play me some merry dump, to comfort me.

First Musician
  Not a dump we; 'tis no time to play now.

Peter
  You will not then?   110

First Musician
  No.

Peter
  I will then give it you soundly.

First Musician
  What will you give us?

Peter
  No money, on my faith, but the gleek; I will give you
  the minstrel.   115

First Musician
  Then will I give you the serving-creature.

Peter
  Then will I lay the serving-creature's dagger on your
  pate. I will carry no crotchets; I'll re you, I'll fa you;
  do you note me?

First Musician
  An you re us and fa us, you note us.   120

Second Musician
  Pray you, put up your dagger, and put out your wit.

125–127 An excerpt from a song by Richard Edwards, "In Commendation of Music."

126 **dumps** sorrows.

129 **Catling** Peter is making up the last names of the musicians; a catling is a lute string of catgut.

131 **Rebeck** three-stringed fiddle.

134 **Soundpost** peg supporting the body of a stringed instrument.

136 **cry you mercy** beg your pardon.

138 **sounding** playing.

143 **stay** stay for.

Peter

Then have at you with my wit! I will dry-beat you with
an iron wit, and put up my iron dagger. Answer me like
men :

> "When griping grief the heart doth wound   125
>   And doleful dumps the mind oppress,
> Then music with her silver sound"—

Why "silver sound"? why "music with her silver
sound"?—What say you, Simon Catling?

First Musician

Marry, sir, because silver hath a sweet sound.   130

Peter

Pretty! What say you, Hugh Rebeck?

Second Musician

I say, "silver sound," because musicians sound for
silver.

Peter

Pretty too! What say you, James Soundpost?

Third Musician

Faith, I know not what to say.   135

Peter

O, I cry you mercy; you are the singer: I will say for
you. It is "music with her silver sound," because musicians have no gold for sounding:

> "Then music with her silver sound
>   With speedy help doth lend redress."   140

> [*Exit.*

First Musician

What a pestilent knave is this same!

Second Musician

Hang him, Jack! Come, we'll in here; tarry for the
mourners, and stay dinner.

> [*Exeunt.*

3 **bosom's lord**   that is, heart.

7 **gives . . . leave**   allows.

11 **shadows**   images.

18 **monument**   burial vault.

21 **took post**   traveled by post horse.

23 **office**   duty.

ACT V

Scene 1. Mantua. A street

Enter Romeo.

Romeo
> If I may trust the flattering truth of sleep,
> My dreams presage some joyful news at hand:
> My bosom's lord sits lightly in his throne,
> And all this day an unaccustom'd spirit
> Lifts me above the ground with cheerful thoughts.   5
> I dreamt my lady came and found me dead—
> Strange dream, that gives a dead man leave to think!—
> And breath'd such life with kisses in my lips,
> That I reviv'd and was an emperor.
> Ah me! how sweet is love itself possess'd,   10
> When but love's shadows are so rich in joy!

> *Enter Balthasar, booted.*

> News from Verona! How now, Balthasar!
> Dost thou not bring me letters from the friar?
> How doth my lady? Is my father well?
> How fares my Juliet? that I ask again;   15
> For nothing can be ill, if she be well.

Balthasar
> Then she is well, and nothing can be ill:
> Her body sleeps in Capels' monument,
> And her immortal part with angels lives.
> I saw her laid low in her kindred's vault,   20
> And presently took post to tell it you:
> O, pardon me for bringing these ill news,
> Since you did leave it for my office, sir.

41 **weeds** clothing.
   overwhelming that is, overhanging.
42 **Culling** sorting.
   simples medicinal herbs.

47 **account** number, reckoning.

49 **packthread** wrapping twine.
   cakes of roses caked rose petals (used for perfume).

53 **present** immediate.

Romeo

    Is it e'en so? then I defy you, stars!

    Thou know'st my lodging: get me ink and paper,   25

    And hire post-horses; I will hence tonight.

Balthasar

    I do beseech you, sir, have patience:

    Your looks are pale and wild, and do import

    Some misadventure.

Romeo

                Tush, thou art deceiv'd: 30

    Leave me, and do the thing I bid thee do.

    Hast thou no letters to me from the friar?

Balthasar

    No, my good lord.

Romeo

             No matter; get thee gone,

    And hire those horses; I'll be with thee straight.   35

                       [*Exit Balthasar.*

    Well, Juliet, I will lie with thee tonight.

    Let's see for means:—O mischief, thou art swift

    To enter in the thoughts of desperate men!

    I do remember an apothecary,

    And hereabouts a' dwells, which late I noted   40

    In tatter'd weeds, with overwhelming brows,

    Culling of simples; meager were his looks;

    Sharp misery had worn him to the bones:

    And in his needy shop a tortoise hung,

    An alligator stuff'd and other skins   45

    Of ill-shap'd fishes; and about his shelves

    A beggarly account of empty boxes,

    Green earthen pots, bladders and musty seeds,

    Remnants of packthread and old cakes of roses,

    Were thinly scatter'd, to make up a show.   50

    Noting this penury, to myself I said,

    An if a man did need a poison now,

    Whose sale is present death in Mantua,

54 caitiff   miserable.

62 ducats   gold coins.
63 gear   stuff.

66 trunk   body.

70 utters   distributes.

73 starveth   look out hungrily.

Here lives a caitiff wretch would sell it him.
O, this same thought did but forerun my need,   55
And this same needy man must sell it me.
As I remember, this should be the house:
Being holiday, the beggar's shop is shut.
What, ho! apothecary!

    Enter Apothecary.

Apothecary
                        Who calls so loud?   60

Romeo
  Come hither, man. I see that thou art poor;
Hold, there is forty ducats: let me have
A dram of poison; such soon-speeding gear
As will disperse itself through all the veins,
That the life-weary taker may fall dead,   65
And that the trunk may be discharged of breath
As violently as hasty powder fir'd
Doth hurry from the fatal cannon's womb.

Apothecary
  Such mortal drugs I have; but Mantua's law
Is death to any he that utters them.   70

Romeo
  Art thou so bare and full of wretchedness,
And fear'st to die? famine is in thy cheeks,
Need and oppression starveth in thy eyes,
Contempt and beggary hangs upon thy back,
The world is not thy friend, nor the world's law: 75
The world affords no law to make thee rich;
Then be not poor, but break it, and take this.

Apothecary
  My poverty, but not my will, consents.

Romeo
  I pay thy poverty and not thy will.

Apothecary
  Put this in any liquid thing you will,   80

88 **cordial**   restorative (a substance which has a stimulating effect upon the heart).

6 **associate**   accompany.

8 **searchers**   health officers.

12 **stay'd**   stopped.

And drink it off; and, if you had the strength
Of twenty men, it would dispatch you straight.

Romeo

There is thy gold, worse poison to men's souls,
Doing more murder in this loathsome world,
Than these poor compounds that thou mayst not sell: 85
I sell thee poison, thou hast sold me none.
Farewell: buy food, and get thyself in flesh.
Come, cordial and not poison, go with me
To Juliet's grave; for there must I use thee.

[*Exeunt.*

Scene 2. *Friar Laurence's cell*

Enter Friar John.

Friar John

Holy Franciscan friar! brother, ho!

Enter Friar Laurence.

Friar Laurence

This same should be the voice of Friar John.
Welcome from Mantua: what says Romeo?
Or, if his mind be writ, give me his letter.

Friar John

Going to find a barefoot brother out,   5
One of our order, to associate me,
Here in this city visiting the sick,
And finding him, the searchers of the town,
Suspecting that we both were in a house
Where the infectious pestilence did reign,   10
Seal'd up the doors and would not let us forth;
So that my speed to Mantua there was stay'd.

18 **nice**   trivial.
   charge   weight, importance.

21 **iron crow**   crowbar.

26 **beshrew**   censure, blame.
27 **accidents**   happenings.

Friar Laurence
Who bare my letter then to Romeo?

Friar John
I could not send it—here it is again—
Nor get a messenger to bring it thee,   15
So fearful were they of infection.

Friar Laurence
Unhappy fortune! by my brotherhood,
The letter was not nice, but full of charge
Of dear import, and the neglecting it
May do much danger. Friar John, go hence;   20
Get me an iron crow and bring it straight
Unto my cell.

Friar John
Brother, I'll go and bring it thee.

                                                [*Exit*.

Friar Laurence
Now must I to the monument alone;
Within this three hours will fair Juliet wake: 25
She will beshrew me much that Romeo
Hath had no notice of these accidents;
But I will write again to Mantua,
And keep her at my cell till Romeo come:
Poor living corse, clos'd in a dead man's tomb!   30

                                                [*Exit*.

Scene 3. A churchyard; in it a monument

belonging to the Capulets

Enter Paris and his Page, bearing flowers and a torch.

Paris
Give me thy torch, boy: hence, and stand aloof:
Yet put it out, for I would not be seen.

3 **all along**   at full length.

11 **adventure**   take the risk.

14 **sweet**   perfumed.
15 **wanting**   lacking.

20 **cross**   thwart.

22 **mattock**   a digging tool.

Under yond yew trees lay thee all along,
Holding thine ear close to the hollow ground;
So shall no foot upon the churchyard tread,   5
Being loose, unfirm, with digging up of graves,
But thou shalt hear it: whistle then to me,
As signal that thou hear'st something approach.
Give me those flowers. Do as I bid thee, go.

Page

[*Aside*]   I am almost afraid to stand alone   10
Here in the churchyard; yet I will adventure.

> [*Retires.*

Paris

Sweet flower, with flowers thy bridal bed I strew—
   O woe! thy canopy is dust and stones—
Which with sweet water nightly I will dew,
   Or, wanting that, with tears distill'd by moans: 15
The obsequies that I for thee will keep
Nightly shall be to strew thy grave and weep.

> [*The Page whistles.*

The boy gives warning something doth approach.
What cursed foot wanders this way tonight,
To cross my obsequies and true love's rite?   20
What, with a torch! Muffle me, night, a while.

> [*Retires.*

*Enter Romeo and Balthasar, with a torch, mattock,
and a crow of iron.*

Romeo

Give me that mattock and the wrenching iron.
Hold, take this letter; early in the morning
See thou deliver it to my lord and father.
Give me the light: upon thy life, I charge thee,   25
Whate'er thou hear'st or seest, stand all aloof,
And do not interrupt me in my course.
Why I descend into this bed of death
Is partly to behold my lady's face,

32 **dear** important.
33 **jealous** suspicious.

44 **doubt** suspect.

45 **maw** stomach.

48 **despite** defiance.

But chiefly to take thence from her dead finger   30
A precious ring, a ring that I must use
In dear employment: therefore hence, be gone:
But if thou, jealous, dost return to pry
In what I farther shall intend to do,
By heaven, I will tear thee joint by joint   35
And strew this hungry churchyard with thy limbs:
The time and my intents are savage-wild,
More fierce and more inexorable by far
Than empty tigers or the roaring sea.

Balthasar

I will be gone, sir, and not trouble you.   40

Romeo

So shalt thou show me friendship. Take thou that:
Live, and be prosperous: and farewell, good fellow.

Balthasar

[*Aside*]   For all this same, I'll hide me hereabout:
His looks I fear, and his intents I doubt.
                                                  [*Retires.*

Romeo

Thou detestable maw, thou womb of death,   45
Gorg'd with the dearest morsel of the earth,
Thus I enforce thy rotten jaws to open,
And in despite I'll cram thee with more food.
                                        [*Opens the tomb.*

Paris

This is that banish'd haughty Montague
That murder'd my love's cousin, with which grief,   50
It is supposed, the fair creature died,
And here is come to do some villainous shame
To the dead bodies: I will apprehend him.
                                        [*Comes forward.*
Stop thy unhallow'd toil, vile Montague!
Can vengeance be pursu'd further than death?   55
Condemned villain, I do apprehend thee:
Obey, and go with me; for thou must die.

Romeo

    I must indeed, and therefore came I hither.
    Good gentle youth, tempt not a desperate man;
    Fly hence and leave me: think upon these gone;   60
    Let them affright thee. I beseech thee, youth,
    Put not another sin upon my head,
    By urging me to fury: O, be gone!
    By heaven, I love thee better than myself,
    For I come hither arm'd against myself: 65
    Stay not, be gone: live, and hereafter say,
    A madman's mercy bid thee run away.

Paris

    I do defy thy conjurations
    And apprehend thee for a felon here.

Romeo

    Wilt thou provoke me? then have at thee, boy!   70

                             [*They fight.*

Page

    O Lord, they fight! I will go call the watch.

                                  [*Exit.*

Paris

    O, I am slain! If thou be merciful,
    Open the tomb, lay me with Juliet.

                               [*Dies.*

Romeo

    In faith, I will. Let me peruse this face:
    Mercutio's kinsman, noble County Paris!   75
    What said my man, when my betossed soul
    Did not attend him as we rode? I think
    He told me Paris should have married Juliet:
    Said he not so? or did I dream it so?
    Or am I mad, hearing him talk of Juliet,   80
    To think it was so? O, give me thy hand,
    One writ with me in sour misfortune's book!
    I'll bury thee in a triumphant grave;
    A grave? O, no, a lantern, slaughter'd youth;

86 **feasting presence** festive reception room for royal affairs of state.

89 **keepers** nurses.
90 **lightning** lightening of the spirit.

115 **dateless** eternal.
 engrossing buying up in gross, monopolizing.
116 **conduct** guide.

For here lies Juliet, and her beauty makes   85
This vault a feasting presence full of light.
Death, lie thou there, by a dead man interr'd.
                              [*Laying Paris in the tomb.*
How oft when men are at the point of death
Have they been merry! which their keepers call
A lightning before death: O, how may I   90
Call this a lightning? O my love! my wife!
Death, that hath suck'd the honey of thy breath,
Hath had no power yet upon thy beauty:
Thou are not conquer'd; beauty's ensign yet
Is crimson in thy lips and in thy cheeks,   95
And death's pale flag is not advanced there.
Tybalt, liest thou there in thy bloody sheet?
O, what more favor can I do to thee
Than with that hand that cut thy youth in twain
To sunder his that was thine enemy?   100
Forgive me, cousin! Ah, dear Juliet,
Why art thou yet so fair? shall I believe
That unsubstantial death is amorous,
And that the lean abhorred monster keeps
Thee here in dark to be his paramour?   105
For fear of that, I still will stay with thee,
And never from this palace of dim night
Depart again: here, here will I remain
With worms that are thy chambermaids; O, here
Will I set up my everlasting rest,   110
And shake the yoke of inauspicious stars
From this world-wearied flesh. Eyes, look your last!
Arms, take your last embrace! and, lips, O you
The doors of breath, seal with a righteous kiss
A dateless bargain to engrossing death!   115
Come, bitter conduct, come, unsavory guide!
Thou desperate pilot, now at once run on
The dashing rocks thy seasick weary bark.
Here's to my love.   [*Drinks.*]   O true apothecary!
Thy drugs are quick. Thus with a kiss I die.   120
                              [*Dies.*

121 **speed**   protector.
122 **stumbled at graves**   an ill omen.

125 **vainly**   uselessly.

*Enter, at the other end of the churchyard, Friar
Laurence, with a lantern, crow, and spade.*

Friar Laurence
 Saint Francis be my speed! how oft tonight
 Have my old feet stumbled at graves! Who's there?

Balthasar
 Here's one, a friend, and one that knows you well.

Friar Laurence
 Bliss be upon you! Tell me, good my friend,
 What torch is yond that vainly lends his light   125
 To grubs and eyeless skulls? as I discern,
 It burneth in the Capels' monument.

Balthasar
 It doth so, holy sir; and there's my master,
 One that you love.

Friar Laurence
                    Who is it?   130

Balthasar
                              Romeo.

Friar Laurence
 How long hath he been there?

Balthasar
                              Full half an hour.

Friar Laurence
 Go with me to the vault.

Balthasar
                          I dare not, sir: 135
 My master knows not but I am gone hence;
 And fearfully did menace me with death,
 If I did stay to look on his intents.

Friar Laurence
 Stay, then; I'll go alone: fear comes upon me;
 O, much I fear some ill unlucky thing.   140

150 unkind   unnatural.

153 comfortable   comforting.

167 timeless   untimely.

Balthasar

   As I did sleep under this yew tree here,
   I dreamt my master and another fought,
   And that my master slew him.

Friar Laurence

                        Romeo!

                              [*Advances.*

   Alack, alack, what blood is this, which stains   145
   The stony entrance of this sepulcher?
   What mean these masterless and gory swords
   To lie discolor'd by this place of peace?

                         [*Enters the tomb.*

   Romeo! O, pale! Who else? what, Paris too?
   And steep'd in blood? Ah, what an unkind hour   150
   Is guilty of this lamentable chance!
   The lady stirs.

                            [*Juliet wakes.*

Juliet

   O comfortable friar! where is my lord?
   I do remember well where I should be,
   And there I am: where is my Romeo?   155

Friar Laurence

   I hear some noise. Lady, come from that nest
   Of death, contagion and unnatural sleep:
   A greater power than we can contradict
   Hath thwarted our intents: come, come away:
   Thy husband in thy bosom there lies dead;   160
   And Paris too: come, I'll dispose of thee
   Among a sisterhood of holy nuns:
   Stay not to question, for the watch is coming;
   Come, go, good Juliet; I dare no longer stay.

Juliet

   Go, get thee hence, for I will not away.   165

                      [*Exit Friar Laurence.*

   What's here? a cup, clos'd in my true love's hand?
   Poison, I see, hath been his timeless end:

168 **churl**   miser.

178 **attach**   arrest.

184 **woes**   pitiful bodies.
185 **ground**   basis.
186 **circumstance**   details.
    descry   discern.

O churl! drunk all, and left no friendly drop
To help me after? I will kiss thy lips;
Haply some poison yet doth hang on them,   170
To make me die with a restorative.

                                            [Kisses him.

Thy lips are warm.

First Watchman
   [*Within*]   Lead, boy: which way?

Juliet
   Yea, noise? then I'll be brief. O happy dagger!

                           [Snatching Romeo's dagger.

This is thy sheath; there rust, and let me die.   175

        [Stabs herself, falls on Romeo's body, and dies.

   Enter Watch, with the Page of Paris.

Page
   This is the place; there, where the torch doth burn.

First Watchman
   The ground is bloody; search about the churchyard:
   Go, some of you, whoe'er you find attach.
   Pitiful sight! here lies the county slain;
   And Juliet bleeding, warm, and newly dead,   180
   Who here hath lain this two days buried.
   Go, tell the prince: run to the Capulets:
   Raise up the Montagues: some others search:
   We see the ground whereon these woes do lie;
   But the true ground of all these piteous woes   185
   We cannot without circumstance descry.

   Reenter some of the Watch, with Balthasar.

Second Watchman
   Here's Romeo's man; we found him in the churchyard.

First Watchman
   Hold him in safety, till the prince come hither.

   Reenter Friar Laurence, and another Watchman.

192 **a great suspicion** a very suspicious thing.

199 **startles** starts up.

208 **mista'en** mistaken, gone astray.
house the dagger's sheath.

Third Watchman
Here is a friar, that trembles, sighs and weeps:
We took this mattock and this spade from him,   190
As he was coming from this churchyard's side.

First Watchman
A great suspicion: stay the friar too.

Enter the Prince and Attendants.

Prince
What misadventure is so early up,
That calls our person from our morning rest?

Enter Capulet, Lady Capulet, and others.

Capulet
What should it be that they so shriek abroad?   195

Lady Capulet
The people in the street cry Romeo,
Some Juliet, and some Paris, and all run
With open outcry toward our monument.

Prince
What fear is this which startles in our ears?

First Watchman
Sovereign, here lies the County Paris slain;   200
And Romeo dead; and Juliet, dead before,
Warm and new kill'd.

Prince
Search, seek, and know how this foul murder comes.

First Watchman
Here is a friar, and slaughter'd Romeo's man,
With instruments upon them fit to open   205
These dead men's tombs.

Capulet
O heavens! O wife, look how our daughter bleeds!
This dagger hath mista'en, for, lo, his house

212 **warns** summons.

221 **mouth of outrage** immoderate clamoring.

227 **of suspicion** suspected.

230 **make against** implicate.
231 **impeach** accuse.
    purge clear.

Is empty on the back of Montague,
And it missheathed in my daughter's bosom!   210

Lady Capulet

O me! this sight of death is as a bell
That warns my old age to a sepulcher.

Enter Montague and others.

Prince

Come, Montague; for thou art early up.
To see thy son and heir more early down.

Montague

Alas, my liege, my wife is dead tonight;   215
Grief of my son's exile hath stopp'd her breath:
What further woe conspires against mine age?

Prince

Look, and thou shalt see.

Montague

O thou untaught! what manners is in this,
To press before thy father to a grave?   220

Prince

Seal up the mouth of outrage for a while,
Till we can clear these ambiguities,
And know their spring, their head, their true descent;
And then will I be general of your woes,
And lead you even to death: meantime forbear,   225
And let mischance be slave to patience.
Bring forth the parties of suspicion.

Friar Laurence

I am the greatest, able to do least,
Yet most suspected, as the time and place
Doth make against me, of this direful murder;   230
And here I stand, both to impeach and purge
Myself condemned and myself excused.

Prince

Then say at once what thou dost know in this.

234 date of breath time of life.

253 borrow'd temporary.

260 closely secretly.

Friar Laurence
    I will be brief, for my short date of breath
    Is not so long as is a tedious tale.   235
    Romeo, there dead, was husband to that Juliet;
    And she, there dead, that Romeo's faithful wife:
    I married them; and their stol'n marriage day
    Was Tybalt's doomsday, whose untimely death
    Banish'd the new-made bridegroom from this city;   240
    For whom, and not for Tybalt, Juliet pin'd.
    You, to remove that siege of grief from her,
    Betroth'd and would have married her perforce
    To County Paris: then comes she to me,
    And with wild looks bid me devise some means   245
    To rid her from this second marriage,
    Or in my cell there would she kill herself.
    Then gave I her, so tutor'd by my art,
    A sleeping potion; which so took effect
    As I intended, for it wrought on her   250
    The form of death: meantime I writ to Romeo,
    That he should hither come as this dire night,
    To help to take her from her borrow'd grave,
    Being the time the potion's force should cease.
    But he which bore my letter, Friar John,   255
    Was stay'd by accident, and yesternight
    Return'd my letter back. Then all alone
    At the prefixed hour of her waking
    Came I to take her from her kindred's vault,
    Meaning to keep her closely at my cell   260
    Till I conveniently could send to Romeo:
    But when I came, some minute ere the time
    Of her awaking, here untimely lay
    The noble Paris and true Romeo dead.
    She wakes, and I entreated her come forth,   265
    And bear this work of heaven with patience:
    But then a noise did scare me from the tomb,
    And she, too desperate, would not go with me,
    But, as it seems, did violence on herself.

271 **privy**   secretly cognizant of.

278 **post**   posthaste, with all speed.

284 **rais'd**   roused.

All this I know; and to the marriage   270
Her nurse is privy: and, if aught in this
Miscarried by my fault, let my old life
Be sacrific'd some hour before his time
Unto the rigor of severest law.

Prince

We still have known thee for a holy man.   275
Where's Romeo's man? what can he say in this?

Balthasar

I brought my master news of Juliet's death,
And then in post he came from Mantua
To this same place, to this same monument.
This letter he early bid me give his father,   280
And threaten'd me with death, going in the vault,
If I departed not and left him there.

Prince

Give me the letter; I will look on it.
Where is the county's page, that rais'd the watch?
Sirrah, what made your master in this place?   285

Page

He came with flowers to strew his lady's grave;
And bid me stand aloof, and so I did:
Anon comes one with light to ope the tomb;
And by and by my master drew on him;
And then I ran away to call the watch.   290

Prince

This letter doth make good the friar's words,
Their course of love, the tidings of her death:
And here he writes that he did buy a poison
Of a poor 'pothecary, and therewithal
Came to this vault to die and lie with Juliet.   295
Where be these enemies? Capulet! Montague!
See, what a scourge is laid upon your hate,
That heaven finds means to kill your joys with love!
And I, for winking at your discords too,
Have lost a brace of kinsmen: all are punish'd.   300

302 **jointure**   dowry.

307 **at such rate be set**   be so highly valued.

Capulet
O brother Montague, give me thy hand:
This is my daughter's jointure, for no more
Can I demand.

Montague
               But I can give thee more:
For I will raise her statue in pure gold;   305
That whiles Verona by that name is known,
There shall no figure at such rate be set
As that of true and faithful Juliet.

Capulet
As rich shall Romeo's by his lady's lie;
Poor sacrifices of our enmity!   310

Prince
A glooming peace this morning with it brings;
   The sun for sorrow will not show his head:
Go hence, to have more talk of these sad things;
   Some shall be pardon'd and some punished:
For never was a story of more woe   315
Than this of Juliet and her Romeo.

                                 [*Exeunt.*

READER'S GUIDE

Barbara Brandt

Teacher of English
Newtown High School
New York City

INTRODUCTION

Shakespeare's *Romeo and Juliet* is the most famous of all love stories and probably, too, the greatest of all tales of young, romantic love.

What explains the enduring appeal that this play has had for audiences and readers for almost 400 years? Is that appeal explained alone by the mutual love between Romeo and Juliet, a love that is an inspiring ideal of perfection in its purity, innocence, and selflessness?

Shakespeare's art is never that simple. This play is not only a great love story. More than any other of Shakespeare's plays, *Romeo and Juliet* is packed with action, speed, excitement, tension. It breathes and pulses with life. It bubbles, seethes, glows, burns.

As you read the play, you will want to learn to understand and appreciate more deeply its unique qualities of greatness. The *Reader's Guide* will help you to do so. You will be asked to explore questions under two topics:

Conflict!
Appreciating Shakespeare's Art

Before you begin to read the play and deal with the *Reader's Guide* problems, read the following explanatory comments on each of these topics.

CONFLICT!

The world of *Romeo and Juliet*, like the real world, is filled with the excitement and tension of conflict, contradiction, oppositeness. Here there are violence and crime versus peace and law; the old versus the young; understanding versus hate; true love versus infatuation; spiritual love versus physical love; fate versus free will; selfishness versus sacrifice; courage versus fear; tragedy versus humor; trust versus suspicion; parents versus children; life versus death; marriages versus funerals; dark versus light; and night versus day. Finally, there is the ideal and the perfect world that man aspires to—as represented by the mutual love of Romeo and Juliet—versus the real and disharmonious world that man lives in.

The poet Shelley wrote that

> Life, like a dome of many-colored glass,
> Stains the white radiance of Eternity.

We may compare the "white radiance" to the pure love between Romeo and Juliet. But, that perfect light can be seen only as it shines through the bits and pieces of the many-colored glass dome of life. Though it is imperfect, there is dazzling excitement and beauty and variety in the stained-glass dome, and so it is with this play.

The questions under this heading will direct your attention to the conflicts, the clash and interaction of oppositeness that make *Romeo and Juliet* a racy, exciting play. Particular stress will be placed on the exploration of two themes, *love and hate* and *man and fate*.

Love and Hate

When most people think of *Romeo and Juliet*, they immediately associate the play with young, romantic love, but the play concerns itself with exploring a much wider range of human affections. It focuses not only on the bonds of love between Romeo and Juliet, but also upon the guise of love-infatuation, upon familial love, and upon the related affectionate feelings involved in friendship and loyalty and trust.

We are all painfully aware that bonds of love and friendship are not the only emotional forces in our lives. These positive feelings compete to assert themselves in a world where their opposites—hatred and enmity—also flourish. Every day we see evidence of man's wish for love, peace, and harmony challenged or thwarted by the strong forces of aggression, ill-will, and envy.

Love and hate do not exist simply, in a side by side fashion, independent of one another. In fact, the relationship between them can be very complicated indeed. The pursuit of one, for instance, can ironically lead to the practice of the other; men go to war to insure peace; people hurt others in the name of love.

In *Romeo and Juliet*, Shakespeare examines the forces of love and hate. He not only depicts for us the struggle of love to develop and survive in a hostile environment, but also illustrates the complicated effects that these opposite emotions have upon each other and upon our lives.

Man and Fate

For thousands of years men have looked to the stars in order to acquire information about the future. In this respect, the modern man who consults his daily horoscope in the local newspaper in order to know the wisest course of action to follow for the day is no different from the ancient Greek seeking the aid of an oracle or the medieval man turning to his astrologer for advice. The faith exemplified in all of these actions is based upon the belief that there is some force in the universe—call it fate or predestination or the will of the gods—outside the control of man which determines and prescribes the course that events in the universe shall follow.

Opposed to this age-old view is the belief that man himself creates his own destiny—that is, by virtue of his actions, his choices, and his character, man has responsibility for his own future. Shakespeare himself expresses this position in his play *Julius Caesar* when he has Cassius, one of the leading characters, say that "The fault . . . is not in our stars but in ourselves, that we are underlings." Here the conviction is clearly stated that man's position in society is the result not of fate ("the stars") but of personal choice and endeavor.

Romeo and Juliet (written a few years before *Julius Caesar*), however, opens on a different note; it reflects the opposite opinion of the role of fate in man's life. The opening speech, the Prologue, refers to Romeo and Juliet as "starcross'd lovers," a phrase which suggests that they were doomed from the beginning by a malign fate.

Since Shakespeare has expressed both views, let us see in the course of reading how much of the tragedy is the result of adverse fate and how much can be attributed to mistakes in judgment or personal faults within the characters themselves. To make a determination, we will have to analyze the characters, know the kind of people they are, evaluate the course of action they choose to follow, and, at the same time, we will have to consider those events which remain outside human control and appear to be the workings of an evil design in the universe.

APPRECIATING SHAKESPEARE'S ART

Romeo and Juliet, like all of Shakespeare's plays, is written in poetry, and its lines abound in masterful examples of the techniques which lend poetry its power and its beauty. Shakespeare the poet makes us see and hear and feel through the artistic use of the one tool he has at his disposal—words. He creates word pictures (images) to make us respond emotionally, or he uses words or comparisons which have particularly strong associations to guide the way we feel. Let us see how Shakespeare uses these techniques by examining Romeo's reaction when he beholds Juliet for the first time. He says:

> It seems she hangs upon the cheek of night
> Like a rich jewel in an Ethiop's ear;

As we read these lines, the word *Ethiop* leads us to conjure up in our imaginations the picture of an exotic person, alluring and mysterious. The image, thus, suggests Romeo's interest, his desire to penetrate the secret of Juliet's identity. Juliet's loveliness is enhanced further by the comparison of her person to "a rich jewel," an object that has value, beauty, desirability. That Romeo reacts sensually to the sight of Juliet is revealed in yet another comparison—as the jewel hangs upon the ear of the Ethiopian, so Juliet seems to hang upon "the cheek of night"; here the softness of the face and the sensuousness of the evening are suggestive of Romeo's emotional state.

Upon close examination of *Romeo and Juliet,* we begin to notice that there is a predominance of techniques which rely upon the quality of oppositeness for their effectiveness. The imagery, for example, frequently evokes pictures of light and dark; the settings alternate in scenes of day and night; the dialogue often contains the intermingling of humor and gravity.

The language, too, is marked by this same property. Often, contradictory ideas are combined in a single phrase (we see this exemplified in one of the most famous lines of the play—"parting is such *sweet sorrow"*) and contradictory statements are joined in one sentence, as when Capulet remarks that "it is so very late, / That we may call it early by and by." Single words, also, are often invested with double meanings through the device of punning. Sampson's and Gregory's toying with the words "choler," mean-

ing anger, and "collar," meaning hangman's noose, in the opening scene is but one example.

Just as Shakespeare the poet employs techniques which de-
pend upon the interplay of opposite meanings and situations,
Shakespeare the dramatist uses a related device to develop his
story. He presents us with information of which the characters
themselves are ignorant. As a consequence, when we listen to
Romeo and Juliet speak, we know the truth to be the opposite of
their assumptions, and, as we watch them attempt to pursue their
desires, we know that the outcome will be the opposite of their
dreams; more specifically, as we, the readers or viewers, behold
the flowering of Romeo and Juliet's love, we know, because we
have previously been told, how transient the lovers' happiness
will be. This technique, known as dramatic irony, intensifies our
involvement with the characters, makes us experience the ways
in which the world—the sum total of the bits and pieces of the
mosaic of glass—affects the characters' attempt to preserve their
love, their "white radiance."

In *Romeo and Juliet*, then, subject matter and technique unite
in a common purpose. Not only does the play deal with a story
of conflicting opposites, but the writing itself becomes a rein-
forcement of that theme. The questions in this section of the
Guide, therefore, will lead you to appreciate and enjoy the ways
in which Shakespeare's poetic and dramatic skills add to the
power of the play.

QUESTIONS

Act I, Scene 1

CONFLICT!

1. In the Prologue, a basic conflict in the play is introduced.

a. How do the Capulets and Montagues (the "two households") behave toward one another? Which line describes their behavior?

b. According to the Prologue, how does the behavior of the Capulet and Montague children compare to their elders'?

c. Immediately following the Prologue we see a dramatization of the behavior described there. How does the brawl begin?

d. Who else becomes involved in the fray?

2. What reason does each of the following have for fighting or attempting to participate in the brawl: Sampson, Abram, Benvolio, Tybalt, Capulet, Montague?

3. To what extent do any of the characters exhibit signs of remembering or caring about the original cause of the feud? What does this indicate about the current hatred?

4. Find two phrases in the Prologue which suggest that fate is responsible for the tragedy which befalls Romeo and Juliet. Underline the word which specifically refers to the role of fate. *Example:* "A pair of <u>star-cross'd</u> lovers."

5. To what extent do the events in this scene indicate that the feuding appears to be motivated by an evil fate? Justify your response with specific reference to events in the play.

6. What steps does the prince take to end the disturbance and prevent future outbreaks? Why does he feel so severe a measure necessary?

7. What contrast is provided by the reactions of Benvolio and Tybalt when each comes upon the street fight?

8. Why do both Lady Capulet and Lady Montague oppose their husbands' rushing into the fight? Which line best expresses their reason?

9. Sandwiched between the ominous forecast of the Prologue and the overt hostility of the brawl is an exchange between Capulet's servants, Sampson and Gregory. How does the character of their conversation contrast with the rest of the scene?

10. What mutual lack of understanding does there appear to be in the relationship between Romeo and his parents? (Consider lines 141–150.)

11. In this scene we view the effects of Romeo's current love interest.

    a. What strange behavior have his parents noticed?

    b. What other feelings does Romeo experience in conjunction with love?

    c. To what extent is Romeo aware that his behavior is abnormal?

    d. Why has being in love resulted in odd behavior and negative feelings?

    e. How deep do you think Romeo's love is? Support your judgment with evidence from the scene. What is Benvolio's opinion?

12. What signs of immaturity do you notice in Romeo's behavior?

APPRECIATING SHAKESPEARE'S ART

13. Unburdening himself to Benvolio, Romeo describes his feelings about love in a list of comparisons. (lines 189–193)

    a. What properties does love share with smoke?

    b. What other comparisons reveal negative feelings about love?

    c. In what way does the last comparison, "a preserving sweet," provide a contrast to the others we have considered? What does its placement at the end of the list reveal about Romeo's attitude toward his experience of love?

14. Romeo's conflicting reactions to love are reflected in his choosing words which have conflicting meanings to express his emotions.

a. What does Romeo mean when he says, "I live dead"? (line 225)

b. What opposing words does Romeo use to describe the object of his love? (lines 216–217)

c. Reread lines 175–178 in which Romeo describes love with a series of phrases, each embodying a contradiction. Choose one contradiction, for example, "sick health," and explain how both parts of the phrase could be simultaneously true.

15. The prince expresses his displeasure with those men involved in the street brawl (lines 78–80):

> What ho! You men, you beasts,
> That quench the fire of your pernicious rage
> With purple fountains issuing from your veins.

a. What picture does this passage make you envision? Which words contribute most to the vividness of the image?

b. To what does the prince compare the men's reason for fighting?

c. Shakespeare uses the word *fire* again in line 177. Why is this word appropriate to describe both rage and love?

16. Reread Benvolio's and Montague's speeches, lines 113–137. What image does each use to describe the dawning of a new day?

Act I, Scene 2

CONFLICT!

1. Consider the portrait of youth depicted in the first half of this scene.

a. What passage attests to Juliet's youthfulness?

b. What characteristic of youth does this passage emphasize? Which words are particularly effective in suggesting this characteristic?

c. Find in Capulet's conversation two other images of youth.

2. In what respect does Capulet serve as a contrast to the youth of which he speaks? (Consider his statement, "The earth hath swallow'd all my hopes but she.")

3. a. How does Capulet handle Paris's proposal?

b. What does the manner in which Capulet handles Paris's proposal reveal about the kind of father he is?

c. How do you think a different type of father might handle the same situation?

4. The same advice is volunteered by Capulet and Benvolio to Paris and Romeo respectively.

a. What is requested in both instances?

b. In what respect does Paris provide a contrast to Romeo?

5. Reread lines 55–57. What evidence is there in this excerpt that Romeo's words are exaggerations and do not express deeply felt love?

6. To what extent is Romeo's momentous decision to crash Capulet's party the result of chance? Of his own volition?

APPRECIATING SHAKESPEARE'S ART

7. Reread lines 24–30.

a. Find two sets of contrasting images.

b. Who are the "Earth-treading stars"? Why does Capulet find this comparison appropriate to describe them?

8. Which words in the following quotations best convey Benvolio's opinion about Romeo's "love"? Why are they effective?

> Compare her face with some that I shall show,
> And I will make thee think thy swan a crow.

> Take thou some new infection to thy eye,
> And the rank poison of the old will die.

Act I, Scene 3

CONFLICT!

1. As the Nurse indulges herself by rambling on about her memories of Juliet's childhood (lines 19–51), she touches upon several of the bits and pieces of human experience. Find three pairs of contrasting components of life.

2. In the last scene we focused upon Capulet's feelings toward his daughter; in this scene we are given a view of Juliet's relationship with her mother.

    a. Describe the mother-daughter relationship. What evidence in the scene provides the basis for your description?

    b. In what respect is the Nurse's reaction to the proposal more like a typical mother's?

    c. To whom does Juliet appear to be closer, Lady Capulet or the Nurse? What probably accounts for this preference? Cite lines from the scene which illustrate the nature of Juliet's relationship to her mother and to the Nurse. Explain why you selected each.

3. Notice that Lady Capulet's and the Nurse's characters serve as contrasts to one another.

    a. How do their manners of speaking differ?

    b. What difference in temperament is revealed by their parting words to Juliet? What other example of this difference is contained in the scene?

4. Judging from the events thus far, to what extent do you think Juliet's future remains in her own hands?

APPRECIATING SHAKESPEARE'S ART

5. Speaking of Paris, Lady Capulet declares that "Verona's summer hath not such a flower." In what way do the words "summer" and "flower" enhance her meaning?

6. Reread lines 88–91. What two meanings can be ascribed to each of the following words? (1) the volume; (2) margent [margin]; (3) unbound; (4) cover.

7. The Nurse's parting words to Juliet contain a simply stated contrast, "Seek happy nights to happy days." What happiness does the word day refer to? the word night?

Act I, Scene 4

CONFLICT!

1. Compare Romeo's attitude toward attending Capulet's feast with Mercutio's and Benvolio's. Account for the difference.

2. In what way does Mercutio reveal himself to be a concerned friend of Romeo? How might someone with less regard for Romeo's friendship react to Romeo's mood?

3. To what extent do you think Mercutio would behave as Romeo does if he were rejected by a lady? How might he react?

4. Consider Romeo's last speech in this scene.

   a. What premonition does he have?

   b. On what is his premonition based?

   c. What contrast is provided by Mercutio's opinion of dreams? What "theory" does he spout to explain the content of dreams? To what extent do you agree with his basic viewpoint?

   d. To what extent does Romeo appear to be fatalistic? What other corroborating evidence is there in this scene?

APPRECIATING SHAKESPEARE'S ART

5. In Mercutio and Benvolio's bantering with Romeo, find **(a)** two words that are used as the basis for puns; **(b)** two pairs of words or phrases used as contrast.

6. Consider lines 118–119. To what does Romeo compare himself? Why is the comparison apt?

7. What is the "mire . . . wherein thou stick'st up to the ears" from which Mercutio says he will rescue Romeo? (lines 41–43) In what respect does Romeo's present situation resemble being caught in a swamp?

8. What does Mercutio mean when he refers to dreams as "children of an idle brain"? (line 103)

9. What visual contrast is evident in this scene?

Act I, Scene 5

CONFLICT!

1. a. In what respect does Capulet serve as a contrast to Romeo in this scene?

b. To what does Capulet refer when he says in line 22, " 'tis gone, 'tis gone, 'tis gone"? What causes the shift in his otherwise jocular mood?

2. This scene marks the meeting of the lovers.

a. What is the basis of Romeo's initial attraction to Juliet? Find a line which supports your answer.

b. Why can't this be as viable a motive for Juliet's attraction to Romeo? On what do you think her love is founded?

c. Do you think Juliet has already fallen in love with Romeo before the speech which we hear spoken on stage? Justify your position.

d. Consider the lovers' exchange in lines 96–103. (1) What is the goal of Romeo's flirtation? What ploy does he use to engineer his success?

(2) What obstacles does Juliet put in Romeo's path? Why do you think she does this? What evidence is there that Juliet is as eager to receive the kiss as Romeo is to bestow it?

3. Although chance is largely responsible for Romeo's presence at the feast, and consequently his opportunity to meet Juliet, to what extent is it responsible for Romeo's and Juliet's falling in love?

4. How does Romeo in love compare to Romeo infatuated?

5. What is Tybalt's reaction to the discovery that Romeo is among the guests? Capulet's? Account for the difference. To what extent do you think Capulet's reaction might have resembled Tybalt's if the clock could be turned back forty years?

6. What hint of future complications is contained in Tybalt's parting words (lines 94–95)? On what does he make his prediction? If these complications come to pass, to what extent will Romeo's bad luck have played a role?

7. The lovers' pure joy does not remain untainted for long.

a. How does the happiness of each of them become dampened?

b. With this new knowledge, what options remain open to them? Which alternative do you think most young people in love would choose?

8. How does Juliet's behavior in this scene alter the impression of her character conveyed by her behavior in Scene 3? To what extent do you think Juliet is the type of girl to leave her future intentionally to the whims of chance?

9. Reconsider Romeo's foreboding at the end of the previous scene. To what extent do you think the events in this scene make those forebodings seem prophetic?

10. What strong emotions are experienced by the characters during this scene? In what way does the setting serve to intensify those emotions?

APPRECIATING SHAKESPEARE'S ART

11. Consider the exchange between Romeo and Juliet.

a. To what does Romeo compare Juliet? himself?

b. What opinion of her does this comparison suggest?

12. What techniques does Shakespeare use to express the magnitude of Juliet's beauty in Romeo's eyes? (lines 44–49)

13. After they have parted company, the lovers' speeches abound in contrasts and contradictions. Cite three examples. Why are these contrasts particularly appropriate at this time?

14. If you were directing this scene, how would you keep the audience aware of Romeo and Juliet's developing relationship during the exchange between Capulet and Tybalt?

Act II, Scene 1

CONFLICT!

1. What obstacle to the development of the lovers' relationship does the Prologue underscore?

2. Upon what mistaken assumption do Benvolio and Mercutio base their explanation for Romeo's disappearance? Why is their assumption a reasonable one?

3. Romeo's true motives are markedly opposed to the childishness which his friends attribute to him. What strength in Romeo's character comes to light as a result of his being truly in love? What decision does Romeo make? Why? What are the possible consequences of his decision?

APPRECIATING SHAKESPEARE'S ART

4. In the Prologue the conflict inherent in the lovers' situation is reflected in the choice of words. Find two examples of phrases which are particularly effective because their words exhibit contrast.

5. Mercutio's banter is ironic. However, what misinformation is his banter based upon?

6. The repetition of initial consonants (alliteration) is a technique used by poets. Notice that the sound d is repeated three times in the first line of the Prologue. Find another example of this same technique in the Prologue.

Act II, Scene 2

CONFLICT!

1. The "white radiance" of Romeo and Juliet's love begins to manifest itself.

a. Find a line which illustrates each of the following facets of Juliet's love: (1) the depth of Juliet's love; (2) the honesty and sincerity of Juliet's love; (3) Juliet's willingness to sacrifice anything she has for Romeo; (4) Juliet's concern for Romeo's safety.

b. Find a line which illustrates each of the following facets of Romeo's love: (1) the depth of Romeo's love; (2) Romeo's willingness to endure personal danger for his love's sake; (3) the tender, gentle aspect of Romeo's love; (4) Romeo's worship of Juliet's beauty.

2. Even at this moment of incomparable joy—the discovery that their passions, hopes, and loves are mutually experienced—the "white radiance" is contaminated by "many-colored glass."

a. Along with love, the night air is charged with fear. Find two instances of Juliet's expressing wariness or concern lest they be discovered.

b. Why does Juliet ask herself, "What's in a name?" To what extent do you think changing his name would make Romeo more acceptable to Juliet's family?

c. Even though Romeo and Juliet are each sure of his own feelings, they express fear or concern that somehow the love might not be mutual. (1) What is the basis of Romeo's fears?

(2) What is the basis of Juliet's fears? (Consider: Why does she request that Romeo "swear not by the moon"?)

(3) Given the circumstances thus far, which, if any, of the lovers' fears do you feel are justified? Why?

d. What reservation about the evening's encounter does Juliet express when she compares it to lightning (line 125)? Why does this make her uneasy? Do you think this is a legitimate concern? Why?

e. What effect is produced by Juliet's having to interrupt the meeting with Romeo to respond to her nurse's calls?

3. What hopes for the future do the lovers envision? What plans do they agree upon to help translate their dreams to realities? At this point, do the characters themselves or chance appear to be the force directing the progress of events?

4. Notice that the scene is set at night.

a. What association does the darkness of night usually evoke?

b. What opposite meaning does the night hold for the lovers? Find a line which reveals the importance of the darkness for their interview as exemplified in Romeo's line, "I have night's cloak to hide me. . . ." (line 79)

c. What association does the light of day usually evoke?

d. What meaning does daylight hold for the lovers? Find a line which reveals their attitude toward the approaching light.

APPRECIATING SHAKESPEARE'S ART

5. The multitude of images and comparisons relating to celestial bodies—the sun, the moon, the stars—is particularly appropriate.

a. Why is it very natural that thoughts of the heavens should occur to Romeo?

b. Moreover, what associations do the heavens evoke which make Romeo's dwelling upon them suitable?

6. The scene abounds in contrasting images of light and dark.

a. Find several passages containing references to light.

b. Find several passages containing references to darkness.

c. What function do the images of light seem to serve?

d. What function do the images of darkness seem to serve?

7. The lovers wish to be together not only verbally and spiritually, but physically as well. Find a line which poetically states that desire.

8. Consider lines 139–141.

a. What quality of her love does Juliet find comparable to the sea?

b. What idea which runs contrary to common sense does Juliet express in this excerpt? In what respect can it be true in the instance of Juliet's love?

9. What contradiction is contained in Juliet's assertion that "parting is such sweet sorrow"? (line 198) What truth lives within the seeming contradiction?

Act II, Scene 3

CONFLICT!

1. Friar Laurence's understanding of life includes an appreciation of the conflicts and contradictions suggested by Shelley's image of "many-colored glass." He finds, moreover, that this aspect of human experience has its counterpart in nature.

    a. For each of the following quotations from Friar Laurence's opening speech, identify the opposition which the Friar notes: (1) "The earth that's nature's mother is her tomb." (2) "For nought so vile that on the earth doth live, / But to the earth some special good doth give." (3) "Virtue itself turns vice, being misapplied, / And vice sometime's by action dignified." (4) "Within the infant rind of this small flower / Poison hath residence, and medicine power."

    b. Give an example from your own experience or from current events which illustrates the truth of quotation (3) above.

2. Describe the relationship between Romeo and Friar Laurence. Is the Friar a suitable person for Romeo to turn to?

3. What is the Friar's reaction to the sudden switch in Romeo's affection? How does he reconcile Romeo's success with Juliet and his failure with Rosaline?

4. Why does the Friar agree to perform the marriage in such haste?

5. What contrast in pace is there between the speech and actions of Romeo and the Friar? Which of the Friar's lines best illustrate the contrast between himself and Romeo?

APPRECIATING SHAKESPEARE'S ART

6. Reread the Friar's description of the sunrise. (lines 1–4)

    a. What image does the Friar's description of daybreak evoke?

    b. Which words indicate the Friar's attitude toward day? toward night?

Act II, Scene 4

CONFLICT!

1. What are Mercutio's feelings about Tybalt? Why? To what extent do his reasons seem adequate to you?

2. Mercutio believes that Tybalt's letter to Romeo contains a challenge to a duel.

    a. How does Benvolio feel Romeo will react to the challenge? Mercutio?

    b. Given Romeo's newly found love, how do you think he will react?

3. Mercutio happily notes "Now art thou Romeo." What change has taken place in his friend's behavior to prompt this observation?

4. What evidence do we see in this scene of the Nurse's tender affection and loyalty to Juliet?

5. What plan has Romeo devised to effect the marriage between himself and Juliet? to gain access to his wife while she lives with her parents? To what extent do you think he is adopting a wise course of action? What problems, if any, can you foresee?

6. Although this is predominantly a lighthearted scene, what overtones of seriousness or hints of future complications do you sense?

APPRECIATING SHAKESPEARE'S ART

7. What makes Mercutio's opening remarks about Romeo (lines 4–5) ironic?

8. The Nurse cautions Romeo not to lead Juliet "into a fool's paradise." What kind of happiness does the word "fool's" suggest?

Act II, Scene 5

CONFLICT!

1. The power of this scene lies in the tension which is generated by the contrast between Juliet and the Nurse. Let us discover the nature of that contrast.

a. Consider Juliet's state of mind. (1) For what is she waiting?

(2) How long has she been waiting? To what extent has the Nurse taken an excessively long time to arrive?

(3) What kind of thoughts might likely travel through one's mind in such a situation? Find two lines which reveal some of the thoughts which plague Juliet.

(4) What feelings does she experience between the time she waits and the time she finally receives the message?

b. Consider the Nurse's behavior. (1) How does she respond to Juliet's impatient requests for Romeo's message?

(2) What concerns are uppermost in her mind?

2. Once she receives Romeo's message, to what extent does it seem to Juliet that her happiness will be "radiantly white"?

3. What does Juliet do when she receives Romeo's message? What role has fate played in arranging the impending marriage?

UNDERSTANDING SHAKESPEARE'S ART

4. Consider Juliet's opening speech.

a. What effect does the multitude of short, choppy syllables create?

b. Which words or groups of words are especially effective in conveying Juliet's wishes that the news be delivered with dispatch?

c. What comparison serves as a contrast to Juliet's wish for speed?

5. Juliet prompts the Nurse:

270

Though news be sad, yet tell them merrily;
If good, thou shamest the music of sweet news
By playing it to me with so sour a face.

a. What words are set in opposition to each other?

b. To what does Juliet compare the Nurse?

c. What do music and sweet news have in common?

6. What is the "bird's nest" to which the Nurse refers in line 75?

7. What effect does the use of the homonyms (words that sound the same but have different spellings and meanings) *hie* and *high* have in the last line of the scene?

Act II, Scene 6

CONFLICT!

1. What is the cause of the uneasiness which the Friar expresses in lines 1 and 2? Who does he feel will bear the responsibility if his uneasiness proves to be well founded?

2. On the threshold of marriage, both Romeo and Juliet are burgeoning with exquisite happiness, experiencing only the pure radiance, the all-encompassing passion of their mutual love. Find lines which illustrate the intensity of Romeo's love and joy; of Juliet's.

3. Although the major purpose of this scene is to portray Romeo and Juliet's happiness at its height, there is an opposing undercurrent at work here. Reread lines 9–15.

a. What warning does the Friar give Romeo?

b. To what extent does there appear to be a contradiction in the advice to "love moderately"?

APPRECIATING SHAKESPEARE'S ART

4. To what does the Friar compare intense, unbridled love (lines 9–13)? Why are these comparisons so apt?

5. What contradiction to common sense is contained in the Friar's statement that "too swift arrives as tardy as too slow"? In what special situation does the Friar feel there is truth in this contradiction?

6. What image is evoked by the following lines?

> A lover may bestride the gossamer
> That idles in the wanton summer air,
> And not yet fall.

Which words are particularly effective in creating the feeling that love is an uplifting, delicate, soothing experience?

7. To what extent are you satisfied with Shakespeare's indication that the marriage ceremony will take place offstage rather than his actually staging it for you to behold?

Act III, Scene 1

CONFLICT!

1. Let us consider how Romeo's state of mind at the opening of the scene differs from Mercutio's, Benvolio's, and Tybalt's.

a. From where is Romeo coming? What thoughts are probably occupying him?

b. What is the topic of Benvolio and Mercutio's "discussion" (lines 1–32)? To what extent is this type of exchange typical of the behavior and attitudes of the interactions between these two friends? What information does Benvolio give us which could account for the kind of behavior that occurs here and in the remainder of this scene?

c. For whom are Tybalt and his supporters searching when they chance upon Mercutio and Benvolio? Why?

d. Review your answers to **a**, **b**, and **c**. What contrast is set up between Romeo and the people who surround him in this scene?

2. How has love changed Romeo's outlook on people? reordered his values?

3. Why doesn't Romeo want to accept Tybalt's challenge? Why does he?

4. Consider the reasons for Mercutio's death.

a. On whom does his repeated phrase "a plague o' both your houses" lay responsibility? Why does he feel this way?

b. To what extent must Mercutio himself bear some of the blame?

5. To what extent do you agree with Romeo that his avoidance of the duel was "effeminate" or cowardly? For which Romeo do you have more respect, the pacifist or the avenger?

6. Romeo could have left Tybalt's punishment to the law. What personality trait has he exhibited which precludes his having chosen this course of action?

7. Reread Benvolio's recounting for the Prince of the fatal fight. (lines 153–176)

a. If you knew nothing of the play but this speech, how could you tell with whom Benvolio's sympathy and affections lie?

b. To what extent is this an accurate account?

8. Why does the Prince allow Romeo to escape the fate of death for his crime? What punishment does he mete out instead?

9. To what extent do you blame fate for tarnishing the radiance of Romeo's happiness? To what extent do you blame Romeo himself?

10. What strong point of contrast is there between the highlight of the previous scene and the critical events of this scene?

APPRECIATING SHAKESPEARE'S ART

11. Romeo bemoans the fact that Juliet's beauty "hath... soften'd valor's steel." What two meanings can we assign to the word *steel*?

12. Even as he lay dying, Mercutio could not avoid seizing the opportunity for jest and wordplay (lines 94–96).

a. Which word in the following sentence has a double meaning? What are the two meanings?

Ask for me tomorrow, and you will find me a grave man.

b. What comparisons does he use to describe his fatal wound? What meaning does he wish to convey through those comparisons?

Act III, Scene 2

CONFLICT!

1. Note as we did in earlier scenes the kinds of events which occur at night and those which happen during the day.

    a. What promise does the coming evening hold for Juliet?

    b. What is her attitude toward the daytime in her opening speech?

    c. In the last scene, during what portion of the day did the deaths occur?

    d. To what extent do you find that the play so far has been consistent in portraying happy events in darkness and threatening occurrences in daylight?

2. What effect does knowledge of Romeo's deed have upon Juliet's love? What explanation might there be for her initial reaction (lines 75–87)?

3. How well does the Nurse understand the true nature of Juliet's love? What evidence do you find in this scene to support your view?

4. What effect does Romeo's banishment have upon Juliet's outlook toward the future? What course of action does she propose? To what extent do you think she is serious?

5. What contrasts in emotions are portrayed in this scene?

APPRECIATING SHAKESPEARE'S ART

6. Reread Juliet's opening speech (lines 1–33).

    a. Find a line or group of lines which effectively reveals each of the following: (1) her childlike impatience; (2) her passion; (3) her adoration of Romeo.

b. List the contrasting images you find in this speech.

c. What contrast is there between Juliet's image of night, the "sober-suited matron," and Juliet herself at this moment?

7. Through Shakespeare's artistic use of words and dramatic technique, the confusion and turmoil which Juliet experiences in this scene is intensified.

a. Notice the long list of descriptions which Juliet spouts out in her anger. (lines 75–87) List five of them; what do all of these share in common? Choose one description and explain why it is apt in revealing how Juliet feels at this moment.

b. At which point in the scene is the tension increased through the use of dramatic irony?

c. Reread lines 46–53. What word or words heighten our sense of Juliet's confusion?

8. What does the comparison in lines 112–116 reveal about Juliet's reaction to Romeo's banishment?

Act III, Scene 3

CONFLICT!

1. Let us consider what points of contrast we find in the reactions and behavior of Romeo and the Friar in this scene.

a. Consider Romeo. (1) How does Romeo react upon hearing the Prince's sentence?

(2) Considering his situation, what should he have been doing?

(3) What view does he have of his future?

b. Consider the Friar. (1) What is his reaction to the Prince's sentence?

(2) How does he attack the problem of Romeo's future?

(3) What steps does he take to bring Romeo back to himself?

(4) What ray of hope does he hold out for Romeo?

c. Account for the marked differences in the two characters' reactions to the same problem.

d. To what extent do you agree with Romeo that the Friar might feel and act differently if he himself were in Romeo's place (lines 65–71)?

e. What opposing views on philosophy are revealed in the following quotes? To what extent do you think each point of view appropriate to the character who supports it?

I'll give thee armor to keep off that word;
Adversity's sweet milk, philosophy. . . . (lines 55–57)

       Hang up philosophy!
Unless philosophy can make a Juliet,
Displant a town, reverse a prince's doom. . . . (lines 58–61)

2. What effect does Romeo fear his actions have had on Juliet's love? What convinces him that his fears are unfounded?

3. What course of action is Romeo finally steered toward? Who devises the plan?

4. Scenes 2 and 3 of this act depict Juliet and Romeo's reactions to and handling of a crisis situation. Which character demonstrates greater maturity, greater strength in coping with adversity? Why?

APPRECIATING SHAKESPEARE'S ART

5. For each of the following excerpts explain why the italicized word is particularly apt in conveying the poet's meaning. (Consider what each word suggests and how it furthers our understanding of the action or situation.)

a. "I'll give thee *armor* to keep off that word [banishment]." (line 55)

b. "There on the ground, [is Romeo] with his own tears made *drunk*." (line 85)

c. "Now I have stain'd the *childhood* of our joy." (line 99)

d. "How hast thou the heart . . . To *mangle* me with that word 'banished'?" (lines 49–52)

6. Romeo accuses the Friar (lines 23–24):

        Thou cut'st my head off with a golden ax,
        And smilest upon the stroke that murders me.

What image does the excerpt evoke?

7. What three words are opposed to one another in the following quotation? To whom do all three refer? Explain how one person can be all three at once?

> Unseemly woman in a seeming man!
> Or ill-beseeming beast in seeming both! (lines 118–119)

8. What effect does the changing meaning of the word *seem* have? (lines 118–119)

Act III, Scene 4

CONFLICT!

1. This is the second time we witness marriage arrangements being formulated for Juliet. In both instances, what word would you use to describe the manner in which the arrangements are conceived?

2. Why is Capulet so sure that Juliet will accept the marriage arrangements he has worked out with Paris?

3. To what extent do you think Paris really loves Juliet?

4. What kinds of problems do you think Juliet will have to face as a result of this interview between Paris and her parents? To what extent are these problems of her own making?

5. Of what contrasts in human experience are we made aware in this short scene? What action generates these contrasts?

APPRECIATING SHAKESPEARE'S ART

6. Reconcile the contradiction in Capulet's parting words:

> It is so very very late
> That we may call it early by and by.

7. What knowledge, unrevealed to the characters in this scene, does the reader or viewer possess which accounts for the irony of this scene?

Act III, Scene 5

CONFLICT!

1. As in Act II, Scene 2, the lovers are faced with parting and the problem of saying goodbye. In the first instance, the line that best characterized the feelings of the lovers is "parting is such sweet sorrow." Why is this sentiment inappropriate to describe the emotional climate of the current scene? What line from this scene best captures the conflicting feelings of the lovers about the impending separation?

2. Evidence that the generation gap is not a modern phenomenon can be found in the clash between Juliet and her parents.

a. Consider the Capulets' point of view. (1) Capulet asks his wife: "Have you deliver'd to her our decree?" (line 142) What does the word *decree* reveal about Capulet's notion of his parental prerogatives?

(2) Reread lines 185–196. What unspoken but underlying premises about the relative ability of youth and parents to decide upon important questions affecting youth's future is evident in these lines? What expressed belief provides the basis for this conclusion?

(3) Describe Capulet's reaction to his daughter's refusal to obey. What do Lady Capulet's comments reveal about whether this behavior is typical of Capulet? What factors other than Juliet's willful disobedience might be contributing to such an extreme reaction? To what extent can you sympathize with Capulet?

b. Consider Juliet's position. (1) Why can't she obey her parents?

(2) How does Juliet behave in the face of her father's rage? Why doesn't she engage him in an out-and-out argument?

c. Who, if anyone, do you think is right? Why?

3. Consider the Nurse's advice to Juliet. (lines 223–236)

a. In what direction does she try to steer Juliet?

b. Whom do you think she is trying to protect by prompting Juliet to follow this course of action?

278

c. To what extent do you think she is capable of understanding the depth of Juliet's love and devotion to Romeo? What contrast is there in the characters of Juliet and the Nurse?

4. In this scene we have witnessed Juliet's being deserted, one by one, by all those people she has customarily depended upon. Indulging in a moment of self-pity, Juliet bemoans "that heaven should practice stratagems / Upon so soft a subject as myself!" What evidence is there in this scene that Juliet is not as "soft a subject" as she envisions herself?

5. What premonitions of disaster does Juliet have?

APPRECIATING SHAKESPEARE'S ART

6. List five pairs of contrasting words contained in Romeo and Juliet's farewell. What effect does the prevalence of opposing words have upon your appreciation of the emotional impact of this segment?

7. What visual picture is evoked by the following lines? What contrast does the image provide to the emotions Romeo and Juliet are experiencing?

> Look, love, what envious streaks
> Do lace the severing clouds in yonder east:
> Night's candles are burnt out, and jocund day
> Stands tiptoe on the misty mountain tops.

8. The exchange between Lady Capulet and Juliet is characterized by a multitude of ironic statements. For each of the following quotations from Juliet's speeches, tell first what meaning the line has to Juliet and then what opposite meaning it has to Lady Capulet:

a. "Would none but I might venge my cousin's death!"

b. Indeed, I never shall be satisfied
   With Romeo, till I behold him—dead—
   Is my poor heart so for a kinsman vex'd.

c. Madam, if you could find out but a man
   To bear a poison, I would temper it,
   That Romeo should, upon receipt thereof,
   Soon sleep in quiet.

d.   O how my heart abhors
To hear him nam'd, and cannot come to him,
To wreak the love I bare my cousin
Upon his body that hath slaughter'd him!

9. In Juliet's conversation with the Nurse, find a line which has one meaning to the Nurse and an opposite meaning to Juliet.

Act IV, Scene 1

CONFLICT!

1. For what opposite reasons do Juliet and Paris each seek the aid of Friar Laurence?

2. What appears to be Paris's motive for wanting to marry Juliet? To what extent do you blame him for wishing to marry in such haste?

3. Notice the shift in Juliet's behavior which occurs at line 45. Describe her behavior up to this point in the scene. Describe her behavior in the remainder of this scene. Explain why such a marked contrast occurs.

4. What is Juliet willing to do to keep the pure radiance of her love for Romeo untainted?

5. Consider the Friar's role in determining Romeo and Juliet's future.

   a. What desperate course of action does he prescribe to extricate them from their dilemma?

   b. Evaluate the Friar's plan. To what extent is it wise? practical? moral? What alternative suggestions might he have made?

   c. Do you find fate or Juliet herself responsible for Juliet's following the Friar's advice?

APPRECIATING SHAKESPEARE'S ART

6. Juliet's speech (lines 78–89) abounds in imagery.

  a. Find three images which appeal to your sense of sight.

  b. Find two images which appeal to your sense of hearing.

  c. Find an image which appeals to your sense of smell.

  d. Consider your answers **a, b,** and **c.** What feelings does the excerpt create in the reader?

7. Consider Friar Laurence's speech (lines 90–121) which directly follows the selection discussed in question **6** above. Does the imagery in this excerpt add or contrast to the feelings created by Juliet in the preceding speech? Find two quotations which illustrate your point of view.

Act IV, Scene 2

CONFLICT!

1. Consider Juliet's behavior. What gives us the feeling that she will be able to execute the Friar's plan?

2. What change occurs in Capulet's behavior toward Juliet? What motivated this change? To what extent do you think the change in behavior reflects a change in the quality of Capulet's love for his daughter?

3. Again we find a scene which contrasts markedly with the one preceding it. Tell how this scene differs from the previous one in each of the following areas:

  a. Subject matter.

  b. Range of emotion.

  c. Pace.

APPRECIATING SHAKESPEARE'S ART

4. Consider the final speech of the scene. What makes Capulet's lightheartedness so ironic?

Act IV, Scene 3

CONFLICT!

1. What motive do the Nurse and Lady Capulet impute to Juliet's desire to be alone? What opposite reason impels her?

2. For what purpose will the wedding attire that the Nurse and Juliet are selecting be used?

3. Consider the conflict Juliet experiences as she prepares to drink the potion.

　a. What questions arise in her mind as she holds the vial in her hand?

　b. To what extent is her swallowing the draft a testimony to her love?

　c. Would you admire her more or less if she drank the potion without a second thought? Why?

4. What role does fate play in either aiding or hampering Juliet's administering of the potion?

APPRECIATING SHAKESPEARE'S ART

5. Consider lines 25–59, the end of the scene. Notice how Shakespeare's selection of words and images contribute to Juliet's and the reader's experience of terror.

　a. List, in order of their appearance, words or phrases which are associated with death and fear.

　b. Select three images from Juliet's speech (lines 25–59)—one from the beginning, one from the middle, and one from the end—which contribute to creating the atmosphere of terror.

　c. Review the lists you have compiled in answers to **a** and **b**. As you read from top to bottom, what change do you notice in the character of the words and images? What effect does this produce?

Act IV, Scene 4

CONFLICT!

1. a. What discrepancy is there between the kind of reception Capulet declared he would host to honor his daughter's marriage (Act II, Scene 4) and the kind of reception that appears to be in the making here? What kind of person does this reveal Capulet to be?

b. What dramatic purpose is served by Shakespeare's portrayal of Capulet's high-keyed excitement as he directs the preparation for the lavish party?

2. What extreme contrasts do you notice between this scene and the previous one?

APPRECIATING SHAKESPEARE'S ART

3. What irony is there in the Nurse's warning to Capulet that "Faith, you'll be sick tomorrow / For this night's watching"?

Act IV, Scene 5

CONFLICT!

1. The members of the Capulet household have arisen early and are bustling about excitedly. What do they expect the day to hold in store for them? With what opposite reality must they contend?

2. Reread the Nurse's opening speech. Notice that she becomes aware that something is amiss with Juliet in slow degrees. Select, in order of their appearance in the excerpt, four lines which illustrate the progression in the Nurse's awareness.

3. Although the Nurse, the Capulets, and Paris all lament the "death" of Juliet, they do so differently. Characterize the response of each.

4. The death of a family member is usually an occasion of deeply experienced sorrow; what circumstances make the "death" of Juliet particularly pitiful for those close to her?

5. Blaming death and time, the Capulets cry out against external forces for dealing them this blow; to what extent do you think they have brought their misery upon themselves?

6. Acting in his role as spiritual advisor to the Capulets, the Friar attempts to console the mourning family with the seemingly contradictory thought that "nature's tears are reason's merriment."

a. What are the two different kinds of reactions to death that the Friar refers to?

b. Which reaction does the Friar exhort the family to consider? Why? To what extent do you think it possible for the Capulets to follow the Friar's advice at will?

7. In the Friar's place, to what extent would you be satisfied with the execution of the plan thus far?

APPRECIATING SHAKESPEARE'S ART

8. One of the most moving expressions of grief in the scene is Capulet's:

> Death lies on her like an untimely frost
> Upon the sweetest flower of all the field.

a. What visual picture is created in these lines?

b. In Capulet's view, what qualities does his daughter share with the flower?

9. What truth is there in Capulet's comparison, "Death is my son-in-law, Death is my heir"?

10. Identify the opposition or contradiction in each of the following excerpts. Why is this technique particularly suitable in this scene?

a. "Ready to go, but never to return." (line 37)

b. "Life, living, all is Death's." (line 43)

c. "All things that we ordained festival / Turn from their office to black funeral." (lines 87–88)

Act V, Scene 1

CONFLICT!

1. At the outset of the scene Romeo appears to be lighthearted and optimistic.

a. What is he expecting? Why?

b. To what extent is there any truth to the message he divines from his dream?

c. What causes the sudden reversal in his outlook?

2. What effect has separation had upon Romeo's love? Find a line which justifies your response.

3. When Balthasar reports that he has no communication from the Friar, Romeo replies offhandedly, "No matter!" What mistaken assumption does Romeo make? What difference might the Friar's letter have made?

4. What is Romeo's reaction to the news of Juliet's "death"? To what extent is this reaction in keeping with his previous behavior?

5. What obstacles does Romeo have to overcome in order to procure poison?

6. In acquiescing to Romeo's request for a lethal poison, the apothecary declares, "My poverty, but not my will, consents."

a. What two opposing forces are at odds within the apothecary? Which force triumphs?

b. In what respect does the apothecary's behavior provide a contrast to Romeo's?

7. Why doesn't Romeo take the poison immediately?

8. In pursuing solutions to their problems, both Romeo and Juliet resort to the aid of drugs. What contrasts are there in (1) the manner in which each acquires his dosage, (2) the purpose each seeks to accomplish, (3) the attitude of each toward the taking of the drug?

9. List three images which create an impression of the apothecary's poverty. (lines 39–50)

10. Consider Romeo's request to the apothecary. (lines 62–68) What comparison does he use to illustrate the effect of the poison he wishes to purchase? What particular effect does this comparison suggest?

11. A character's point of view affects the meaning of his statements. Sometimes views which contradict good sense can be understood if one interprets the meaning of the utterance from the speaker's position. (1) For each of the following lines explain why the statement would be senseless if the character's viewpoint were omitted. (2) Justify the validity of the thought by considering the speaker's viewpoint:

    a. "I sell thee poison, thou hast sold me none." (line 86)

    b. "Come, cordial and not poison, go with me." (line 88)

    c. "Then she is well, and nothing can be ill." (line 17)

Act V, Scene 2

CONFLICT!

1. Upon hearing Friar John's report, Friar Laurence exclaims, "Unhappy fortune!" What blow has Friar Laurence's plan been dealt? To what extent do you agree with the Friar that "fortune" rather than human error is responsible?

2. What new plan does the Friar devise to counteract the unlucky turn of events? To what extent does this plan offer a sense of hope?

3. Using the facts revealed in this scene, complete the following sentence three different ways: If only _____, things might have been different. (*Example:* If only *Romeo had received the Friar's message*, things might have been different.)

APPRECIATING SHAKESPEARE'S ART

4. What irony is there in Friar Laurence's greeting, "Welcome from Mantua"?

5. What inconsistency in meaning is contained in Friar Laurence's lament, "Poor living corpse"? Explain the truth contained in the description.

Act V, Scene 3

CONFLICT!

1. The last scene left us with a weak shred of hope. Let us consider what effect the opening of this final scene has upon that glimmer of hope.

    a. Where does the scene take place? What time of day is it?

    b. What emotions are expressed by Paris and his page?

    c. Find three pieces of evidence which indicate that Romeo has had no second thoughts about suicide.

    d. To what extent does the opening of the scene reinforce or weaken the hope extended to us by the Friar?

2. Whose love for Juliet appears to be the stronger—Romeo's or Paris's? Why?

3. When he realizes that it is Paris whom he has slain, Romeo says:

> O give me thy hand,
> One writ with me in sour misfortune's book!

    a. What "sour" fate do both men share?

    b. To what extent is Paris responsible for his own death? Is fate responsible?

4. What treatment does Romeo accord his enemies—the men who attempted to kill him? What other portion of the scene do his actions parallel?

5. The final tragedy might have been avoided had Romeo not made one last error of judgment.

> **a.** What clue does he perceive that could have led him to the conclusion that Juliet is not dead?
>
> **b.** What erroneous explanation does he assume accounts for these signs of life?
>
> **c.** Why is Romeo unable to reach a more logical conclusion?

6. What events or circumstances completely outside the control of Romeo and Juliet contributed to their deaths?

7. What evidence is there in this scene that, like the Nurse, the Friar does not understand the depth and character of Juliet's love for Romeo?

8. The Capulet-Montague feud is finally resolved.

> **a.** What is responsible for the reconciliation of the warring households?
>
> **b.** Assessing the outcome of the feud, the Prince declares (lines 297–298):
>
> > See, what a scourge is laid upon your hate,
> > That heaven finds means to kill your joys with love!
>
> (1) What is the price that the feuding families must pay for their hostilities?
>
> (2) What irony does the Prince note in the culmination of the feud?
>
> **c.** What expressed reason do Capulet and Montague give for erecting golden statues of each other's children? What other reason might they have?

9. Montague calls Romeo "untaught." (line 219) For what reversal of the normal order of human events is he chiding his son?

10. What role did hatred play in bringing about the final tragedy?

11. The play draws to an end with the Prince's assertion that "some shall be pardon'd and some punished." Who, if anyone, do you think is deserving of punishment for his contribution to the tragic outcome? of pardon? Why?

12. What apparent contradiction does the Prince's assertion that "A glooming peace this morning with it brings" contain? Why is it true in the context of the play?

13. In the five days which the play spans, love transforms the characters of both Romeo and Juliet.

a. Specifically, what changes do you note in Juliet? in Romeo?

b. What has inspired these changes?

14. To what extent do you agree with the following statements:

a. The lovers are dead at the end of the play, but the love they shared lives on.

b. The play would be better if it ended happily with Romeo and Juliet reunited.

15. If Romeo and Juliet had a chance to relive their lives, what do you think they might have done differently? Capulet and Montague?

16. The Friar concludes (lines 158–159) that:

> A greater power than we can contradict
> Hath thwarted our intents.

a. What does the Friar mean by a "greater power"?

b. Let us try to discover what the "power" that destroys radiance in this play is.

(1) The play presents us with people who have aspirations, dreams, visions of radiance. What is the dream of the future held dear by Romeo and Juliet? Paris? Capulet?

(2) Why isn't it possible for all of these dreams to come true?

(3) For Romeo and Juliet, Paris, and Capulet, list two facts or events which contribute to the destruction of their dreams.

(4) In the world of the play, why isn't having a dream of ideal perfection and the personal desire to realize that dream sufficient to insure its reality?

APPRECIATING SHAKESPEARE'S ART

17. The scene is pervaded by morbid, repugnant images.

a. List several of them.

b. Reread Romeo's speech. (lines 45–48) To whom or what does each of the following phrases refer?

(1) "Thou destestable maw"; (2) "the dearest morsel of the earth"; (3) "thy rotten jaws"; (4) "with more food."

c. What contribution do these images make to the scene?

18. Romeo wishes to "shake the yoke of inauspicious stars / From this world-wearied flesh."

a. What is a yoke usually used for?

b. What are the "inauspicious stars" which form Romeo's yoke?

c. What will Romeo accomplish by shaking off his yoke?

19. Reread lines 117–118.

a. To what does Romeo compare his death?

b. What is his pilot? Why is the comparison apt?

c. What is Romeo's attitude toward dying? Which words best indicate that attitude?

20. Why does Juliet call the instrument of her death a "happy dagger"?